The Complete Guide to
Perthshire Paperweights:
The Final Years

Super-Magnum Bouquet

The Complete Guide to Perthshire Paperweights: The Final Years

by Colin & Debby Mahoney and Gary & Marge McClanahan

Printed in USA

Credits

Paperweight photos: **Gary McClanahan**
Factory photos: **Perthshire Paperweights Limited**

Layout: **Colin Mahoney**

International Standard Book Number: 978-1507861523

Publisher: **Colin Mahoney**

Preface

Perthshire Paperweights Limited produced classic-style paperweights beginning with the founding of the company in the summer of 1968 and continuing until the factory closed in January 2002. Collectors recognized Perthshire's efforts, and Perthshire's paperweights quickly became some of the most desirable of all modern paperweights.

A reference catalogue of the factory production was needed, and in early 1997 the authors published their first book *The Complete Guide to Perthshire Paperweights*. That text documented Perthshire Paperweights Limited's production from 1968 through the 1997 Annual Collection. It was quickly adopted as the standard reference for Perthshire paperweights. Shortly after the factory closed, collectors began asking for an updated version covering production from mid-1997 through the final weights made before the factory closed in 2002.

This book is intended as a companion to the first book and follows the format established therein. The two books, when used in conjunction, catalogue all of the standard production designs made by Perthshire Paperweights Limited during their 34 years of operation.

Acknowledgments

The authors would like to thank all those who contributed information and documentation or loaned paperweights so that the photographic record could be complete.

Neil Drysdale
Richard Giles
Peter McDougall
Leslie Smith

John Charles Cowie
Jim Lachlan
Ian Mailer
Calum McDougall
Frances McDougall
Robert McDougall
Roselyne Mow
Jacqueline Scott
Duncan Smith
Gordon Taylor
Marilyn Williamson
Charles Young

Table of Contents

Annual Collection

Christmas Weights

Limited Edition and
General Range

Special Editions

One-of-a-Kind Weights

Related Items

Perthshire Paperweights
Collectors Club

Picture Canes

Dedication

This book is dedicated to Neil Drysdale. Neil was the heart and soul of Perthshire Paperweights, having taken over the helm when its founder, his father, Stuart Drysdale passed away in August 1990. Neil learned much about the business and easily cultivated friendships among the collectors, paperweight dealers, and other paperweight artists. Neil was a fun-loving person and easy to get to know. He enjoyed life and all it had to offer. He started as a lawyer (solicitor) in Scotland, so the business aspects of the paperweight business came naturally to him. Neil was also a very talented man in his own right. He loved sports (golf, skiing and curling) and was talented at those. He was also an avid gardener, cultivating all sorts of plants (fruits, vegetables, and flowers), enjoying that hobby to its fullest. So, it was a natural thing for him to develop an awareness and appreciation for the beauty of the paperweights the Perthshire factory produced.

For Neil, there was the artistry of the paperweights to try to enhance, the business to run, and the collectors to please. The authors also remember how much Neil cared for the artists and other employees that worked at Perthshire Paperweights. We asked Neil once why Perthshire didn't produce more of one kind of weight and less of other kinds. Neil replied that it was his concern to have all the employees totally employed all year. The Perthshire annual production line always kept in mind what could be done and by whom so that all employees were equally needed and thus employed. It was impressive to us that Neil would care so much about the employees. Many employers do not. In a business where some factories might consider hiring and firing based on trends in an industry, Neil cared about his employees first.

Neil passed away unexpectedly in April of 2001. He was survived by his wife, Jane; two sons, Mark and Lewis from his first marriage to Miriam; two stepdaughters; and his mother, Sigrid Drysdale. He is sadly missed by all including the employees of the former factory. The business could not continue without Neil. He truly was its heart and soul.

Introduction

Collecting glass paperweights has become increasingly popular, and with the growth of the internet and publication of several new paperweight reference books, the collector has many new opportunities to view glass paperweights of all types. Certainly the paperweights produced by Perthshire Paperweights Limited located in Crieff, Scotland, rank high in artistic merit, creativity, and technical excellence and are thus highly prized by collectors everywhere.

The previous book *The Complete Guide to Perthshire Paperweights* presented for the first time complete documentation, in words and pictures, of all of the production designs issued by the factory from the time it formed in 1968 through the date of publication in the spring of 1997. However, the factory continued to produce paperweights and the collectors had no comprehensive reference to Perthshire's production since the 1997 publication.

This book fills that need and is designed as a companion to and continuation of *The Complete Guide to Perthshire Paperweights*, and therefore much of the information contained in that book is **not** repeated in this book, such as:

- Older signature types
- Paperweight base cuttings
- Specific pictorial examples relating to certain Glossary terms
- A more detailed history of Perthshire Paperweights Limited

- Production techniques ("Sand to Art")
- A complete photographic catalogue of designs produced before mid-1997 and not continued after that (such as the illustrated PP64).

PP64

- Some of the "how to" examples included in the *Identification* section of the original book.

Some *Limited Edition and General Range* designs changed several times before 1997 and those pre-1997 variations are not pictured here.

Some of the *Identification* section, including the "how to" examples illustrated in the earlier book, has been updated with current examples. The original chart of "Limited Edition and General Range Production Years" has been updated and is included in its entirety.

After seeing an article about classic antique paperweights in a *Woman's Day* magazine, Stuart Drysdale, then manager of Strathearn Glass, wanted to establish a goal of creating modern paperweights that were of the same classic designs and quality found in antique paperweights. The *Historical Timeline* section allows the reader to follow Perthshire's progress from the first Annual Collection paper-

1969A
The first Annual
Collection design

weight in 1969 through more complex designs as the Perthshire team did indeed meet that stated goal.

Just as the first book was written to be a collectors' reference, this book presents the complete catalogue, in words and pictures, of all of the factory production designs made since midyear 1997. For continuity this book follows the format established in the first book. The *Catalogue* section includes all of the designs that were issued beginning with the 1997 Midyear Edition (shown in the *Special Editions* category) and continuing through the final production year of 2001—and those designs planned and produced in very limited quantities for 2002.

The factory closed in January 2002, and although the 2002 designs were never officially issued, some were indeed produced and sold. Many of these were unfinished, with rough pontil marks, nicks in the surface, and, in some cases not faceted, although the official design was intended to be faceted. However, with the help of Perthshire's Factory Manager, Peter McDougall, the only 2002 collection completed by the factory as it would have been released was obtained. These were the weights made and photographed for the annual

2002G
From the last
Annual Collection

factory catalogue that was never published, and would also have been used for marketing in the late fall of 2001. These factory-produced 2002 weights are included in the respective catalogue categories, along with some unfinished samples that illustrate some possible variations that the collector might encounter.

Unfinished 2002 PP47
(The official design
was faceted.)

Paperweights assigned a letter designation, including the Little Gem weights are included in the *Annual Collection* category.

The *Special Editions, One-of-a-Kind,* and *Related Items* categories include some designs which were produced before 1997. Some of these are not dated, but may be encountered by the collector. Many special editions were made by the factory for various special events, museums, and dealers over the course of the factory's history. There were no specific factory records documenting each edition, so this book documents as many special editions as possible.

In 1997 Perthshire established the Perthshire Paperweights Collectors Club. Paperweights and related objects available only to club members are documented in a separate *Perthshire Paperweights Collectors Club* category.

Perthshire was well-known for its many silhouette and colored picture canes. A new section illustrates many of these. As many canes as possible have been shown as they appear in paperweights; however, some examples were only available as loose canes and are included to make this section as complete as possible. Due to the large number of designs made, often in limited quantities and/or for a specific customer, the collector may find examples not pictured herein.

To ensure accuracy and the correct Perthshire factory designations for the paperweights in this book, factory representatives including Peter McDougall and, before his untimely death, Neil Drysdale, were consulted. The designs and pictures in this book have been carefully compared with Perthshire's published literature. Many of the individual customers who had special editions made exclusively for them were also contacted to verify designs and confirm attributions.

Although there is no question that some design variations exist, and that there are many one-of-a-kind weights that are not represented, it is believed that the weights in this book are a complete documentation of all of the official Perthshire factory production designs that were made between midyear 1997 and the closing of the factory in January 2002. Further, when this book is used in conjunction with *The Complete Guide to Perthshire Paperweights*, the collector will have the most complete and comprehensive guide to all of the Perthshire production designs ever made.

Historical Timeline

This section illustrates the progress of Perthshire Paperweights Limited, beginning with the very first weights made when the company was formed in 1968, and continuing through the very last never-released design.

Additionally, although Perthshire maintained that their weights were a result of a team effort, and therefore did not generally acknowledge individuals, a few of the people who made Perthshire the great paperweight factory that it became are identified. There is no doubt that with the incredibly wide variety of paperweights that were made, and the techniques required to make them, that Perthshire became and remained for many years, the premier paperweight factory in the world.

Much of the information included herein was extracted from the texts of a series of lectures given to collector groups by Neil Drysdale. Readers who would like a more detailed history of Perthshire Paperweights Limited are directed to the History section of the first book *The Complete Guide to Perthshire Paperweights*.

1967

Even before Perthshire Paperweights Limited came into being, the goal for the future factory was established. Stuart Drysdale, then Manager of Strathearn Glass, saw the July 1965 issue of *Woman's Day* magazine that featured an article on classic antique paperweights. Mr. Drysdale showed the article to some of the workers at Strathearn, and they in turn said, "We can do that." Thus the goal to create modern paperweights in the style of and rivaling the quality of the classic antiques was established.

1968

Perthshire Paperweights Limited came into being in the summer of 1968 when Stuart Drysdale left Strathearn over a disagreement about the artistic direction that the company should take. Stuart

Modernistic Strathearn

wanted to pursue designs that followed the classic antique French weights, and Teacher's Whiskey, Strathearn's owners, wanted to pursue a more modernistic style.

Shortly after Mr. Drysdale left Strathearn, a few of the Strathearn workers came to him and suggested that he could form his own company to make paperweights in the classic style. These were Jack Allan, Roy McDonald, and Peter McDougall. John Deacons had already left Strathearn to work with Joe Cowie who built furnaces, and John also joined as one of the original members of the new Perthshire team. Several weeks later Anton Moravek, a Czechoslovakian glass cutter (faceter) joined as well. These then, were the first workers of the new Perthshire Paperweights Limited.

An old abandoned school building was leased and converted into a glass works, and production began in July 1968. The first weights were General Range millefiori designs similar to those that had been made at Strathearn, but of significantly higher quality. These classic concentric millefiori designs became some of the mainstays of Perthshire's production and were given the designations PP1, PP2, and PP3 (varying in size with the PP1 being the largest). The PP1 and PP2, although slightly modified over the years, were still in production when the factory closed 34 years later. The PP3 was discontinued after 1998.

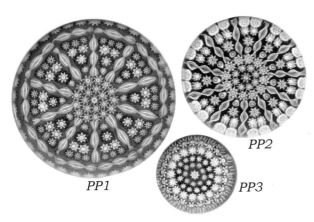

PP1 *PP2* *PP3*

1969

Perthshire produced the first of what was to become the Annual Collection weights—a red/white/blue crown weight in the style of the classic antique St. Louis crown weights. This first Annual Collection weight was marketed through the late Alan Tillman, a very well-known London paperweight dealer. Mr. Tillman was also responsible for introducing Perthshire to the U.S. market. The crown was a success and 258 pieces were sold (out of an edition size limited to 350).

1969A

In addition to this first Annual Collection weight, Perthshire also started the tradition of Limited Editions. These designs were usually millefiori, although a few pieces through the years included both millefiori and lampwork, or occasionally were only lampwork. These were made for only one year, or in some cases over several years, but limited to a specific

number of pieces for each year. These Limited Edition weights were signed and dated. The unlimited General Range designs were sometimes signed but not dated.

Perthshire also began the custom of signing some of these Limited Edition weights with a letter of the alphabet to indicate the year of production, and not with the "P" or "P" with a date signature cane. The PP14 design was the only one to have weights signed with all 26 letters of the alphabet beginning with "A" for 1969 and continuing through "Z" for 1994.

PP14Z

Ryder Cup

Perthshire also made their first Special Edition weight in 1969—a design created for the Ryder Cup Golf event.

Experimentation with colored picture canes began and for the first time several colored picture canes were included in at least one scattered millefiori weight dated 1969.

Colored picture canes of a heart, flower and thistle along with a P1969 date cane (bottom)

1970

The 1970 Annual Collection was expanded to include two weights: the 1970B Flash Overlay, and Perthshire's first lampwork weight, the 1970A Dragonfly. The overlay weight was made by Jack Allan and cut by Anton Moravek. It was produced with six different overlay

colors, and each was scratch-signed on the bottom with the initials "JA" (for Jack Allan) and "AM" (for Anton Moravek). The combined edition size of all colors was 150 pieces.

1970B

This was one of the very few Perthshire weights ever made where the individual makers got to sign the weights.

Although Jack Allan was a talented glassworker, he did not have the skills required to do lampworking, so Angus Hutchinson, who was working as a technical/industrial glass blower for a company in Perth, was recruited to become Perthshire's first lampworker. After experimenting with some colored leaves and flower petals, Angus made the first Perthshire lampwork weight, the 1970A Dragonfly.

1970A

1971

1971A

The 1971 Annual Collection included another flash overlay piece by Jack Allan and Anton Moravek. This time it was an overlay bottle that demonstrated Moravek's faceting ability.

A garlanded lampwork flower on lace which was a major step up from the 1970 lampwork piece and a ribbon crown were also part of the 1971 collection. Once again, the crown was signed with Jack Allan's "JA" cane. This year also marked the production of the first Christmas weight, a tradition that was continued annually (except for 1973) all the way through the last year of production in 2001.

1972

Perthshire's first basket weight was the 1972 Annual Collection "C" Miniature Flower. This design was made as an issue of 1000 pieces, the largest Annual Collection design Perthshire ever made, and all 1000 were sold. By then the lampwork department had expanded in both size and ability, and a pink dahlia with 85 individual petals made in the style of the classic St. Louis antique dahlia weights was produced as part of the collection. This edition of 200 pieces also was fully sub-

1972A

scribed. In fact, Perthshire weights had become so popular in just four years that all three of the 1972 Annual Collection designs were sold out—a total of 1500 pieces.

1973

This was a significant year for Perthshire with many firsts. In fact, every weight in the 1973 Annual Collection incorporated a first for Perthshire. The 1973A design was Perthshire's first

1973A

hollow weight, a white lampworked glass swan inside of a clear hollow faceted weight that was done in acknowledgment of the classic and highly prized antique Baccarat hollow weights.

The 1973B design was a lampwork flower set on a double spiral latticinio cushion. Although many classic antique paperweights included spiral latticinio cushions, those were all single spiral— that is, the latticinio threads started at the bottom center of the weight and spiraled upward in one direction as a series of parallel threads. When viewed from the top, these threads appear to cross, but it was only an illusion as can be seen by viewing the weight from the side. Perthshire somehow figured out how to do a true double spiral, where pairs of threads each start from a single point and spiral upward around the cushion in both directions, and actually cross. Again, a side view confirms this

Double *Single*

unusual technique. To this day, Perthshire—and the Perthshire factory manager who worked in his own studio until he retired in 2012 —appear to be the only ones who have made a true double spiral latticinio.

The 1973C weight was Perthshire's first millefiori closepack paperweight. (The PP15 bottle, first made in 1969, had a closepack in the bottom and in the stopper.) This ever-popular design concept was to be repeated and expanded throughout the production years.

The 1973D was their first carpet ground weight, but more importantly, it was the first use of "picture" or "figure" canes as a major design element in a production weight. Perthshire had been experimenting with silhouette and colored picture canes from the very beginning. The topping cane in the 1971C ribbon crown contains a color picture cane of a flower, and three colored picture canes were previously illustrated in the 1969 text of this section.

Picture canes have always been popular extras in paperweights, from the classic Baccarat Gridel figures to the "running rabbits" of the New England Glass Company. With this 1973D weight, Perthshire started what was to become almost a trademark for them.

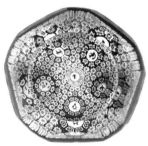

1973D

Picture canes, both colored pictures and silhouettes, became so popular that many collectors began to collect the picture canes for their own interest. In

Bird picture cane

fact, these became such a major collectible in their own right that an entire section of this book has been devoted to illustrating most (but probably not all) of the incredible variety of Perthshire's picture canes that began with the ones made for this 1973D weight—and expanded to include well over 400 different designs.

It is interesting to note that, unlike the cast or molded figure canes such as the Baccarat Gridels, Perthshire used lampwork, torchwork, and crimp techniques to produce many of these earlier canes.

The first picture canes for the 1973 weight were made by lampworker Angus Hutchinson. He was probably the person who made the picture canes for the earlier experimental weights.

Later, as the designs evolved to highly complex colored pictures, a "build" process was used. (This later technique is discussed in the Picture Canes section of this book and also in the earlier book *The Complete Guide to Perthshire Paperweights*.)

For the fifth, and final design in the 1973 collection, Perthshire for the first time ventured into bottom decoration beyond the basic "star cut." This weight had a grid-cut bottom, and Perthshire went on to do various other bottom cuts throughout the years, including diamond, strawberry, and feather cutting.

1974

The popularity of the silhouette/picture canes that appeared in the 1973 weights gave Perthshire the incentive to expand and develop this concept, and in the 1974D weight, Perthshire included a colored picture cane in the design. This

Flower picture cane

was not simply a silhouette cane made with a single-colored glass like the Baccarat Red Devil, but a true colored picture of a flower with red petals and green leaves.

Angus Hutchinson and his team of apprentice lampworkers were also expanding their knowledge of the classic paperweight designs, and a three-flower bouquet weight with hovering dragonfly was made part of the collection.

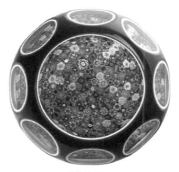

1974E

Millefiori was not neglected. The 1974E was Perthshire's first double overlay weight, a closepack set on a cushion within a double overlay of purple over white.

The 1974 Christmas weight showed Perthshire's dedication to the colored picture cane concept and featured a large picture cane of an English robin topping a green and white crown. Many collectors consider this 1974 colored robin cane to be one of the finest picture canes Perthshire ever made.

Robin picture cane

1975

In 1975 a second hollow weight was produced—this time a penguin on an ice floe within a flash overlay. The 1975D design, a butterfly with millefiori wings made of stretched millefiori canes in the style of the classic Baccarat butterflies,

1975D

was Perthshire's first butterfly weight. Again the concept proved popular and similar butterflies were incorporated into later designs.

1976

Innovation and experimentation continued, and in 1976 Perthshire presented their versions of two classic antique designs—the nosegay and the moss ground.

New techniques produced a spiral cut double overlay butterfly weight and an unusual two-level millefiori cushion design where a fully enclosed lower layer of millefiori canes can be seen through a center opening in the upper layer.

1976D

Another first was the use of colored lace in two of the Limited Edition designs.

PP13

The PP12, which had been a design set on white lace over a colored ground, was made with blue lace, and the PP13 was made with pink lace.

1977

The first triple overlay weight was made with layers of yellow over white over pink encasing a lampwork flower. Another two-layer design was made, this time with a large colored picture cane of a rooster on the lower layer, visible through an opening in the center of the upper opaque cushion.

1977C

1978

The lampworking department continued to grow, both in size and ability, and a weight with a bouquet of complex flowers was made part of the Annual Collection. But this time, there was a wide variety of flowers used and it is possible to find ten or more weights of this 1978D design with no two flowers the same.

Although Perthshire continued to emphasize the team concept over the individual, some of the 1978 double overlay weights with a loop garland design enclosing six colored picture canes were signed with John Deacons "JD" cane in addition to the Perthshire "P" cane. This was in recognition that John, who was an apprentice glassworker when he joined the company in 1968 as one of the original workers, had by now, become a master glassworker in his own right and was now Perthshire's head craftsman.

But the honor was moot, for in mid-1978 John left Perthshire to form his own company. His departure was only the first of several key personnel changes that were to occur over the next few years.

1979

By now the various Perthshire teams had become quite proficient, and the 1979 collections showcased the many talents of each team. The

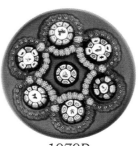

1979D

collection included a complex lampwork bouquet, a hollow weight with a flash overlay, a faceted flash overlay bottle with matching lampwork flowers in the base and stopper and done in two different color overlays, and a garland weight with seven different colored picture canes that varied from weight to weight so many more than just seven picture canes had to be designed.

1980

Late 1979 through 1981 became a time of major transition for Perthshire. John Deacons, the head craftsman, had left in 1978 to form his own company. Alan Scott, who had joined Perthshire as an apprentice lampworker and had progressed to become a full-fledged member of the lampworking team, also left to join John Deacons. Angus Hutchinson, the head lampworker who had been with the company since 1970 decided it was time to retire, and he too left the company. Although the loss of all of these key people could have been catastrophic, Perthshire's apprentice program now proved its worth and new hands picked up the mantel.

Peter McDougall, who had joined the new company as an apprentice in 1968, was now able to have more freedom in design development, and he quickly demonstrated his talents. Heather Crawford, who had joined the company straight from school, was now the head lampworker and she was assisted by a young apprentice named Duncan Smith. Duncan had joined Perthshire in 1978 at age 16.

This new team quickly took charge, and the 1980 Annual Collection included Perthshire's first fruit weight, a three-color swirl, a garland weight featuring

1980D

colored picture canes depicting various forms of transportation and six other designs to make the 1980 collection the largest Perthshire ever made with nine different designs. The Limited Edition weights for 1980 and 1981 are also considered to include some of the most interesting millefiori designs to have been made.

1981

The new team performed well, and the 1981 Annual Collection included a lampwork acorn weight and an encased crown with a latticinio basket set on the top (both designed by Peter McDougall). Also included was one of the most highly prized of all Perthshire weights, the honeycomb-faceted bees weight, where

1981G Bees

Bottom showing four bees

three (and later four) lampwork bees set at the bottom of the weight are reflected in the faceting to create the appearance of a swarm.

A millefiori closepack within a double overlay of amber over white was produced. However, the cutting/faceting varied from four to six side facets, and the top facet was round on some weights and scalloped on others.

11

Wedding Crown

Prince of Wales Feathers

In addition to the weights produced as part of the regular production, 1981 was the year of the Royal Wedding of Prince Charles and Lady Diana. To commemorate this event, Perthshire created two special commemorative weights—a crown with a colored date plaque on the top, and a Prince of Wales Feathers weight.

1982

A 1982 Annual Collection weight continued the colored picture canes theme, this time with nursery rhyme figures. Both Baccarat and St. Louis had made Pompon/Chrysanthemum flowers during the Classic period, and in 1982 Perthshire added a pompon weight to their inventory.

1982G

1983

In 1983 Perthshire accomplished one of the most challenging of all paperweight techniques, the torsade, and what better place for it than surrounding a closepack. That year they also produced the most expensive production weight they ever made, a magnum Gingham weight in honor of the antique St. Louis Gingham that had recently sold for an unheard of price. Once again it was Peter McDougall who was called on to make this masterpiece, and the fancy cutting

and faceting required to make the Gingham design was done by Peter's brother, Barry. The Perthshire Gingham was limited to only 20 pieces and quickly sold out at the issued price of $4,000.

1983 Gingham

1984

The entire 1984 Annual Collection presented a wide range of paperweight techniques including crowns, latticinio cushions, and an unusual caterpillar weight. At first glance, the red/green/black caterpillar appears to be lampwork, but close inspection reveals that it is actually made of

segments of millefiori cane set sideways and joined to form the caterpillar.

The 1984 hollow weight with a lampwork squirrel was made with an unusual flash overlay. Four panels of amber flash were separated by wide shallow flute facets to create the unusual appearance. Although the edition size was limited to 200 pieces, only 94 were ever made—the fewest of any Annual Collection design.

1984F

1985

Perthshire's second triple overlay was part of the 1985 Annual Collection. This time it was blue over white over pink with a nosegay at the center. Perth-

One-off fancy cut double overlays

shire had been doing considerable in-house experiments with fancy overlay techniques, and an occasional one-off piece with multiple overlay layers can be found.

1986

In a salute to the classic tradition, the first double-overlay mushroom weight was part of the 1986 collection, as was a strawberry weight. A lampwork flower bouquet weight featured flowers with seashell-ridged petals. Another classic dahlia weight was included, this time a golden dahlia.

1986E

1987

Perthshire continued to improve and the designs were the products of a mature company with highly evolved techniques. A spiral-cut overlay weight, a two-level weight, a hollow weight, and a closepack with many picture canes were popular pieces in the collection.

1987B

1988

A weight with a honeycomb ground, and a second weight with an upright flower

set with honeycomb doilies over a green or ruby ground were part of the 1988 collection. An unusual concept was applied to the classic swirl design, but this time the swirl was on a translucent color ground, thereby adding one more level of Perthshire creativity to the classic paperweight.

1988G

1989

Perthshire had been experimenting with a Double Overlay Encased Double Overlay. In this incredibly difficult design, a regular double overlay weight is made. This is then cooled and faceted/fancy-cut. Next, the weight is reheated, and a thick layer of clear glass is applied. Next, another double overlay is added. The weight is once again cooled, and a final cutting is done. The failure rate was very high (as much as 90%). Although the factory would take orders, no delivery date was ever promised as it often took many attempts to make just one weight. One of these "Double Doubles" was offered at an auction at the 1989 Convention of the Paperweight Collectors Association. It proved so popular that the factory was overwhelmed with orders—most of which were never filled.

Double Double

This technique was further advanced to a Triple Overlay Encased Triple Overlay, and finally to a Quadruple Overlay. The difficult cutting of this incredible weight can only be described as outstanding.

Only one such "Quad" weight was ever made and it is displayed in the permanent collection of the Bergstrom-Mahler Museum of Glass—a donation of a dedicated Perthshire collector.

1990

This was another transitional year for Perthshire. Duncan Smith, who had joined Perthshire in 1978, was now head of the lampworking department. Unlike the earlier flat bouquets, the new bouquet weights were beginning to become very three-dimensional. The top-of-the-line weight in the Annual Collection was a magnum closepack piedouche, and again an individual was permitted to sign the weight. The closepack atop the piedouche includes Peter McDougall's "PMcD" signature cane. Peter's skill with complex millefiori designs was showing.

1990G

But, a major tragedy struck, and in August, Stuart Drysdale, the founder and General Manager, died. His son Neil was not familiar with paperweights or with the company, but it fell to him to pick up the mantle. To his credit, Neil learned quickly and the company prospered under his guidance.

1991

Another first for Perthshire was the 1991C chequerboard or "Chequer" weight with nine picture canes separated by

1991C

blue rods, in the style of the classic and rare Baccarat Chequer.

Another innovative design was a variation on an encased closepack. A small closepack was enclosed within latticinio ribs.

1992

A featured design in the Annual Collection was an overlaid bouquet set on a latticinio basket. This was another McDougall design, but this time it was not Peter, but Calum McDougall, another of Peter's brothers who came up with the design.

1992E

Perthshire made another hollow weight, this time with a panda eating a bamboo shoot.

The crowning achievement in 1992 was the Magnum Closepack. It was the first in what was to become a Special Limited Edition series. This super-magnum closepack was over four inches in diameter and required an incredible number of complex canes to create. These were signed with both the Perthshire "P" cane and Peter McDougall's "PMcD" cane. The edition was limited to 50 pieces and was quickly sold out.

1993

This was a banner year for Perthshire. Duncan Smith had now perfected the techniques required for three-dimensional bouquets. The one in this collection, complete with reflecting facets and a blue flash ground, was an exceptionally attractive design. The Special Limited Edition series continued with another super-magnum millefiori weight, again over four inches in diameter, and this time including a lampwork flower at the center. To celebrate their 25 years in business, Perthshire made a Special Edition Anniversary Weight. This unusual design used half-canes set to form scalloped rings around a center lampwork flower.

25th Anniversary

During his many trips to the U.S., Neil Drysdale had struck up a close friendship with American master paperweight maker Johne Parsley. Neil invited Johne to come to Crieff and work in the Perthshire factory with the Perthshire team, as both collaborator and teacher. During the first visit, discussions ensued about making a collaborative weight. After Johne returned to the U.S., considerable efforts went into the collaboration. Johne made the lampwork which was sent to Perthshire for inclusion in the weights. Johne later returned for another visit to the factory, and the result was the Perthshire/Parsley Piedouche. The

Perthshire/Parsley Piedouche

signature cane in this weight is unique. A "JP" for Johne Parsley was set with a "PM" for Peter McDougall. The placement is such that the two "P"s in the cane align to form "PP" for Perthshire Paperweights. The edition was limited to only 35 pieces, and again quickly sold out.

1994

Proof that the lampwork department had matured was offered in the Special Limited Edition magnum bouquet. The weight was well over 3-1/2 inches in diameter and had 14 flowers in the bouquet. Although the edition was originally limited to 25 pieces, the demand was so great that it was expanded to a limit of 35. However, it took Duncan Smith the entire year to make these complex bouquets, and only 29 were completed.

1994 Magnum Bouquet

1995

The lampwork department had grown to four members, and the 1995 collection included four bouquet weights. However millefiori was not forgotten, and the 1995A weight included an unusual technique using square canes cut in half to form a zigzag border around the center design. Following the tradition that began in 1992,

1995A

another super-magnum millefiori weight was made as the Special Limited Edition—this time with seven colored picture canes at the center.

1995 Special Limited Edition

1996

Another tradition got its start in 1996 with the release of a special weight that

15

Clown Weight

was not part of the regular catalogue. This was the Clown weight, released just before midyear.

1997

Millefiori again took center stage in the form of a magnum mushroom as the Special Limited Edition design. Signed with Peter McDougall's "PMcD" cane, this multi-faceted mushroom weight was a full 3-1/2 inches high and over 3-1/2 inches in diameter. The very large cap contained hundreds of millefiori canes. In recognition of Perthshire's contribution to the paperweight world, the focus of the 1997 convention of the Paperweight Collectors Association, Inc. (PCA) was an exhibit of all of the Perthshire factory production designs beginning with the first weights from 1968 and including those made for the 1997 Annual Collection. Perthshire was also commissioned by the PCA to make a table favor miniature paperweight that was given to each convention attendee. A special PCA cane was made for the center of this weight.

In recognition of this special event, Perthshire exhibited the largest weight they ever made—a super-magnum bouquet weight nearly 5 inches in diameter and containing 23 individual flowers and 9 buds. This weight will join the Stuart Drysdale Memorial Weight and the Quadruple Overlay weight in the Perthshire collection of the Bergstrom-Mahler Museum of Glass.

Following the tradition started with the clown weight in 1996, Perthshire re-

leased their first official Midyear weight in the summer of 1997. These midyear weights were not part of the annual catalogues. Separate flyers were published to show them.

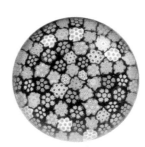

1997 Midyear

1998

Although hollow weights had often been a part of the Annual Collections, the difficulty and expense in making them was such that after 1992 Perthshire would make only one more hollow weight design. The hollow weight containing a very complex lampwork clown figure was included in the 1998 Annual Collection, but at the highest retail price for any Annual Collection weight made to that time. The hollow weight with the clown was priced at $1,000. In a break from tradition, Perthshire also offered the lampwork clown figure as a stand-alone piece that could be purchased separately from the weight.

The Special Limited Edition weight for 1998 was also a departure from the past. During their experimentation with Double Overlay Encased Double Overlay weights, Perthshire made some magnum Encased Double Overlays, similar to the Double Double but without the outer double overlay. These Encased Double Overlay weights had the similar inner double overlay weight, but instead of an outer double overlay, the inner weight was encased in a very thick layer of clear glass. This thick outer encasement was then cut with fancy designs resulting in a brilliant presentation. In the past, Encased Double Overlay weights were only available by special order; however, by 1998 Perthshire felt so confident in their techniques that the Special Limited Edition weight was an Encased Double Overlay design. The edition size was limited to 30 pieces, and although it took the entire year to complete, the edition was sold out.

1998 Special Limited Edition

1999

In 1999 the Midyear Collection was expanded to include six different designs, including a lampwork bouquet. Even though these designs were not included in the regular 1999 factory catalogue when it was published, these weights were given "PP" numbers.

1999 Midyear PP208

2000

The 2000 Annual Collection included an unusual scramble (end-of-day) mushroom weight. The design included five picture canes, and the weight was cut with a top facet and ten side facets. The Special Limited Edition weight was a large lampwork bouquet, but this time with a torsade—a difficult technique that Perthshire had fully mastered.

A special Millennium weight was also included in the catalogue. However, it was not assigned a "PP" number and was only issued for the millennium celebration. It had a special millennium signature cane showing the 2000 date and three stars.

Millennium Weight

A Midyear Collection was made again, also with six different designs including a lampwork bouquet and a blue flower set with millefiori and resting on yellow lace.

2001

Although no one knew it at the beginning of what appeared to be an excellent year for Perthshire, this was to be their final year of production. The Annual Collection was well-received, and included two unusual design concepts. A clear weight containing a small lampwork scene, including a dragonfly and a cattail plant, had a top facet and circular side cuts applied and then the surface area between the side cuts and the top facet was rough-ground giving a frosted look. The rest of the weight remained clear.

2001E

A second design departure was a footed closepack piedouche with the pedestal made with solid-colored panels separated by white stripes instead of the traditional latticinio rods. The foot was faceted with 16 side facets.

Millefiori Ball

The Special Limited Edition weight was a magnum closepack millefiori ball.

The year showed much promise until disaster struck in April. Neil Drysdale, who had taken over after his father's death in 1990, died unexpectedly. This time there was no one to take over. Although Neil had two sons, neither was old enough to assume the responsibility of operating the company. Peter McDougall, now Factory Manager, continued with the daily operations of the factory, but there was no marketing force as Neil had been the marketing contact. Neil's death was a blow that would not be overcome.

Keeping with tradition, Peter ensured that the 2001 Midyear Collection was released. What had started as a single weight in 1997 was now a collection of seven designs.

The struggle to stay in business continued, but on September 11, the terrorist attack on the New York World Trade Center essentially shut down the entire collectibles market worldwide. Suddenly there was no market for paperweights. The outlook for Perthshire's survival became questionable.

In an effort to increase sales, the annual Christmas weight became part of a new Christmas Collection. In addition to the Christmas weight, six designs were included. Four of these, the Little Gems series, were introduced as less expensive pieces limited to only 50. These designs were designated, not with "PP" numbers like preceding midyear weights, but rather with letters like the weights in the Annual Collection. This Little Gem series was planned to be continued in following years.

2001 Little Gems

The other three weights in the Christmas Collection were the 2001 Christmas weight, the PP241 and the "Big and

| 2001 Christmas Weight | PP241 | Big and Bright |

Bright" (PP243 in 2002). Since the 2002 weights were never officially issued, the 2001 Christmas Collection weights were the last official designs produced by Perthshire.

By late 2001 it was becoming apparent that Perthshire's survival was in doubt. To honor its dedicated employees, Perthshire created

Perthshire Staff Weight

one last special edition of 17 weights. However, this time the weights were not made for collectors. Instead, each worker was given one of these Perthshire Staff weights.

2002

Preparations for the 2002 collection were started in late 2001. The designs were picked and a set of weights was made and photographed for the catalogue. But all of this was to no avail. In spite of the excellent quality of the paperweights being made, the market was just not there, and on January 25, 2002, Perthshire closed its doors for the final time.

2002G
Never released

An era was over.

Catalogue

Perthshire classified paperweights into three main factory issued categories—Annual Collection, Limited Edition, and General Range. The Limited Edition and General Range weights have been placed in a single category because they share the numbering system assigned by the factory (PP1, PP2, PP3, etc.). "PP" stands for Perthshire Paperweights and the number indicates the design. The Annual Collection weights are designated by the year and a letter of the alphabet (1998A, 1998B, etc.) per the factory literature.

This book also has categories for items not shown in Perthshire's yearly catalogues. These include Christmas Weights, Special Editions, One-of-a-Kind Weights, and Related Items. A separate category is devoted to paperweights and other items related to the Perthshire Paperweights Collectors Club.

In the years covered by this book, Perthshire also issued some weights designated as Midyear or Midyear Collection. In 2001, the annual Christmas weight became part of a Christmas Collection. However, except for the Midyear weights produced for 1997 and 1998, all of the other Midyear and Christmas Collection weights (except for the actual annual Christmas weight) also had either letter or PP numbers assigned to the design. Therefore those weights are included in either the Annual Collection category (weights designated with an alphabetical letter) or in the Limited Edition and General Range category (weights identified by a "PP" number). The Midyear weights from 1997 and 1998 did not have a factory designation, and these can be found in the Special Editions category.

Annual Collection Weights

Each year Perthshire designed and produced limited editions of a small number of weights designated as the Annual Collection. These weights were usually lampwork or a combination of lampwork and millefiori. A few contained only millefiori. Most Annual Collection weights were signed and dated.

In the Annual Collection category, the weights are arranged by year and include all of the designs designated as the Annual Collection for the years 1998 through 2002. The weights are designated according to the factory catalogue as 1998A, 1998B, etc. Some weights from the 2001 Christmas Collection were named Little Gem  weights, and were also designated by an alphabetical letter (2001H, etc.). The 2002 Annual Collection also included Little Gem weights. Because of the letter designations, the Little Gem weights are included in the Annual Collection category.

2001F

The alphabetical letter assigned to the design usually indicated the relative issue price—*i.e.* the 1998A was issued at a lower price than the 1998B, etc. (Note: The Little Gem weights do not follow this letter/price relationship.)

The current values of Perthshire weights in the secondary market are based on desirability in the eyes of the collector and are unrelated to the letter designation or the original issue price. Because of this market fluctuation, values are not shown for any of the paperweights in this book.

Christmas Weights

Since 1971, with the exception of 1973, Perthshire created a special limited edition Christmas design for each year. Continuing the pattern from the first book, the Christmas designs for 1997 through 2001 can be found in this category. Although the 2001 Christmas weight was part of Perthshire's first and only Christmas Collection, for catalogue purposes, the weights from that collection are included in the appropriate catalogue categories.

1999 Christmas Weight

Limited Edition and General Range

These weights have "PP" number designations and are nearly all millefiori, although a few are lampwork or include a combination of millefiori and lampwork.

General Range weights, such as the PP1, PP2, and PP3, were made over a number of years and are usually signed with a "P" cane, but not dated. Limited Edition weights, which are usually signed and dated, were made only in specific years and in specific edition sizes for each of those years. Examples of these include the PP192, PP193, and PP194. The PP19 is an example of a design produced over several years with a defined edition size each year.

PP19 (2002)

Certain weights underwent design changes from year to year without changing the PP designation. The PP47 is perhaps the best example of this with a radical design change each year, but always retaining the PP47 designation.

PP47 (1998)   *PP47 (2001)*

A chart included in the Identification section shows the years of production as well as the years when the design changed for each PP weight.

Special Editions

Several designs were produced as "Special Editions" of various sizes. Some of these were made to commemorate a specific event such as a Paperweight Collectors Association Convention. Some were made for specific customers such as various paperweight dealers and/or retailers including, but not limited to, G. W. McClanahan, L. H. Selman Ltd., Stone Gallery, Harrods of London, and Lord Jim (a New Orleans retailer).

G.W. McClanahan Butterflies

Specific designs were also made for the Paperweight Collectors Association, Inc., the Yelverton Museum, the Cambridge

Paperweight Circle, and the Bergstrom-Mahler Museum. While a large number of designs are included in this category, it by no means includes them all.

One-of-a-Kind Weights

Perthshire made a wide variety of one-of-a kind (also called "One-Off") weights. Although some were made as design tests or artist proofs, most were made as *tour-de-force* pieces that were too difficult to produce in quantity. These include fancy cut overlays, double overlays, triple overlays, quadruple overlay weights (just one), encased double overlay weights, and unique millefiori and lampwork pieces. A series of paperweights featuring lampwork North American birds was made for the Artists' Fair at the 2001 Paperweight Collectors Association Convention in Corning, New York. Other one-off weights include fancy-cut clear

and overlaid weights in all sizes, and unique highly complex lampwork bouquet weights. Over the years Perthshire produced many one-off weights, and no effort was made to try to include all of them. Instead, this category includes pictures of as many different design concepts as possible by using one or several pictures to illustrate each concept. Although many one-off weights were indeed made during the 1997-2001 time, many of the weights shown in this category were made earlier. However, these rare and unusual works deserve to be included here to illustrate Perthshire's outstanding creative capabilities.

Related Items

Although Perthshire is recognized primarily as a premier paperweight company, they also made many related items, including millefiori and lampwork dishes, vases, and perfume bottles. Examples of these related items, and of a paperweight whimsy are pictured here.

During the late 1980's and early 1990's Perthshire also produced a line of Monart-type glassware that included vases, goblets, dishes, and even lamps. A few of these were sold through dealers; however, most were sold only at the Crieff Visitor Centre. Although these items were not produced during the 1997-2002 period, they were indeed Perthshire production items. As they are not documented elsewhere, their inclusion in this book was important.

Perthshire Lamp

Perthshire Paperweights Collectors Club Items

In 1997 the Perthshire Paperweights Collectors Club was formed. Each member received a small club paperweight upon joining. In each of the following years, a special paperweight was made that was available only to club members. Those weights and the Collectors Club mug are pictured in this category.

1999 Club Weight

Annual Collection

FLOWER ON RADIALS
A pink lampwork flower and six sprigs of leaves set on white latticinio radials over a blue or green ground. Signed with a "P1998" cane in the base. Edition size: 250.

1998A

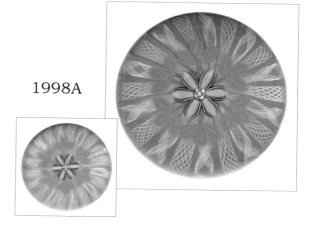

MINIATURE DOUBLE OVERLAY
A small bouquet with flowers, leaves and buds within a double overlay of green over white. One top facet and twelve side facets, and a star-cut base. Scratch-signed "P" on the overlay near the base. Edition size: 200.

1998B

THISTLE
Three thistle flowers and four green leaves set in clear glass in an egg-shaped weight with a frosted exterior. One large front facet and a star cutting at the back. Signed with a "P" cane near the stem. Edition size: 200.

1998C

1998D

GARLANDED PANSY
An amethyst and yellow pansy with leaves surrounded by a garland of red flowers and leaves on a clear ground with a grid-cut or strawberry-cut base. One top facet, five large side facets and ten small side facets. Scratch-signed "P" with the edition number on the base. Edition size: 200.

1998E

ROSE BOUQUET
Two yellow roses and a bud with green leaves surrounded by a garland of blue complex canes, all set on a white latticinio ground. One top facet and twenty-four side facets. Scratch-signed "P" with the edition number on the base. Edition size: 200.

1998F

CUSHION GROUND
A large blue and white lampwork bouquet set on a ruby and black spiral ground. Six picture canes and an outer garland of small canes surround the bouquet. Perthshire literature stated this weight was only domed; however, a number of faceted weights were also made. Signed with a "P1998" cane in the base. Edition size: 200.

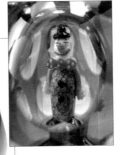

1998G

CIRCUS CLOWN
A circus clown standing in the center of a hollow weight with a ruby flash overlay. One top facet and sixteen side facets. Signed with a "P1998" cane in the base. Edition size: 175.

CIRCUS CLOWN
Lampwork clown with yellow lips, red nose, black derby, red bow and blue gloves. Scrambled millefiori suit with two black buttons and clown feet. This is the clown that was encased in the 1998G hollow weight and was available for separate purchase.

1998G CLOWN

ENCASED DOUBLE OVERLAY
A large bouquet of flowers, buds and leaves on a clear ground within an encased double overlay of blue over white. The overlay is cut with one top facet, six round side facets and six long finger-shaped facets with intricate diamond cutting around the top. The clear encasement is cut with one top facet and twelve side facets. Scratch-signed "P" and the edition number on the base. Edition size: 30.

1998
Special
Limited
Edition

SMALL BOUQUET
A small multicolored bouquet set on a black ground. One top facet and six side facets. Signed with a "P1999" cane in the base. Edition size: 300.

1999A

AQUARIUM
A striped tropical fish swimming among reeds growing from the rock and shell sea bed, all on a turquoise ground. One top facet and five side facets. Signed with a "P1999" cane in the base. Edition size: 200.

1999B

1999C

AMBER FLOWER
A central amber and red flower attached to an encircling garland of buds that ends in another amber flower, all set on a mottled amethyst-red ground. Signed with a "P1999" cane in the base. Edition size: 200.

1999D

UPRIGHT BOUQUET
A small bouquet of purple flowers with yellow stamens and green leaves set on a translucent ruby ground. One top facet and twelve side facets. Signed with a "P" cane at the bottom of the bouquet stem. Edition number inscribed on the base. Edition size: 175.

1999E

BOUQUET ON BLUE
A large bouquet of yellow flowers and purple flowers and buds set on a translucent dark blue ground. One top facet and seven side facets. Signed with a "P1999" cane in the base. Edition size: 175

1999F

THREE-DIMENSIONAL BOUQUET
A large bouquet of blue, pink, amber and amethyst flowers and buds on a clear ground with an unusual feather-cut base. One top facet, eight large and four small side facets. Scratch-signed "P" near the base. Edition size: 150.

DOUBLE OVERLAY

A multicolored bouquet of flowers and buds set on a translucent dark blue ground within a double overlay of amethyst over white, set on a clear foot. One top facet and eighteen side facets to the overlay. Six side flats and a feather-cut base on the clear foot. Scratch-signed "P" on the base. Edition size: 150.

1999G

FOXGLOVE

A large foxglove bloom with several open trumpet flowers and buds on a clear ground with a star-cut base. One top facet and thirty-two side facets. Scratch-signed "P" on the base. Edition size: 25.

1999
Special
Limited
Edition

BOUQUET IN BASKET

A bouquet of two flowers, two buds and green leaves set over a double basket of dark blue canes on the inner basket, and alternating pink and green canes on the outer basket. Flower colors vary. One top facet and five side facets. Scratch-signed "P" on the fire-polished base. Edition size: 250.

2000A

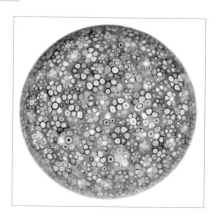

MAGNUM MILLEFIORI

A magnum weight containing more than one hundred complex canes in a closepack design on a white lace ground. Signed "P2000" in canes within the design. Edition size: 200.

2000B

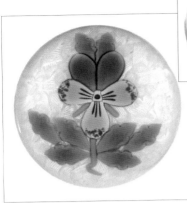

2000C

LARGE PANSY
A large amethyst and yellow pansy with multiple green leaves on a white lace ground. Domed or with one top facet and five side facets. Signed with a "P2000" cane in the base. Edition size: 200.

2000D

FACETED BOUQUET
A three-dimensional bouquet of ruby flowers and buds with green leaves on a translucent dark blue ground. One top facet and twenty-four side facets. Signed with a "P" cane near the base of the stems. Edition size: 200.

2000E

BUDGIES
A pair of wild budgies (birds) on a eucalyptus branch over a clear ground. One top facet and sixteen side facets. Signed with a "P" cane at one end of the branch. Edition size: 175.

2000F

END-OF-DAY MUSHROOM
An end-of-day design pulled down to form a mushroom on a clear ground. Five picture canes are placed within the design. One top facet and ten side facets. Signed "P2000" in canes within the design. Edition size: 175.

LARGE WHITE BOUQUET

Two large white flowers and four large buds forming a bouquet on a clear ground with a star-cut base. One top facet and fourteen side facets. Signed with a "P" cane at the base of the stems. Edition size: 150.

2000G

BOUQUET WITH TORSADE

A three-dimensional bouquet of amethyst, white, and yellow flowers on a clear ground surrounded by a pastel-colored twist forming a torsade. The base is diamond-cut with small "V" cuts around the outside. One top facet and twenty-four side facets. Scratch-signed "P" with the edition number near the base. Edition size: 30.

2000
Special
Limited
Edition

TOCA TOUCAN

A South American Toca Toucan perched on a branch over a clear ground. One top facet and six side facets. Scratch-signed "P" with the edition number near the base. Edition size: 250.

2001A

AMBER BOUQUET

A bouquet of amber flowers and green leaves set on a black ground. One top facet and nine side facets. Signed with a "P2001" cane in the base. Edition size: 150.

2001B

2001C

FLOWER WITH WHITE BUDS
A pink flower surrounded by many branches containing white star cane buds, all on a translucent dark blue ground. Signed with a "P2001" cane in the base. Edition size: 150.

2001D

DAFFODILS
Three yellow daffodil blooms with green stems and leaves over a mottled amethyst-red ground. One top facet and five side facets. Signed with a "P" cane near the base of the stems. Edition size: 175.

2001E

DRAGONFLY
A dragonfly hovering over flowers and reeds growing from a ground of stones, all set in clear crystal with a "V" groove star-cut base. One top facet surrounded by a frosted border. Six interlocking curved grooves and twelve facets around the side. Scratch-signed "P" with the edition number near the base. Edition size: 175.

2001F

SCARLET PIMPERNEL
A large bouquet with three bright red flowers, many buds, leaves and stems set on a clear ground with a star-cut base. One top facet and ten side facets. Scratch-signed "P" with the edition number near the base. Edition size: 150.

MILLEFIORI PEDESTAL
A millefiori closepack design resting on a blue and white pedestal with a clear foot. The foot has sixteen side facets. Signed with a "P" cane within the closepack design. Edition size: 125.

2001G

LITTLE GEM
A bright pink flower and buds on a clear ground with a star-cut base. Some of the star cutting extends part way up the side. One top facet and eight side facets. Signed with a "P" cane next to the base of the stems. Edition size: 50.

2001H

LITTLE GEM
A deep blue flower and buds on a clear ground with a star-cut base. Some of the star cutting extends part way up the side. One top facet and eight side facets. Signed with a "P" cane next to the base of the stems. Edition size: 50.

2001I

LITTLE GEM
A light blue flower and bud on a stem over a black ground. One top facet and many small interlocking side facets extending part way down the side. Signed with a "P2001" cane in the base. Edition size: 50.

2001J

2001K

LITTLE GEM
A white flower with pink and mauve coloring on a stem with green leaves set on an opaque light blue ground. One top facet and forty small side facets. Signed with a "P2001" cane in the base. Edition size: 50.

2001
Special
Limited
Edition

MAGNUM MILLEFIORI BALL
A magnum millefiori weight in the shape of a ball containing hundreds of complex canes. Signed with a "P" cane and a "PMcD" cane within the design. Edition size: 30.

The 2002 Annual Collection was never officially released.

2002A

SWIRL
A turquoise flower with green leaves centered on a swirl of yellow and mauve rods. One top facet and six side facets. Signed with a "P" cane in the base. Edition size: 100/9 made.

2002B

MILLEFIORI AND FLOWER
A central flower surrounded by groups of millefiori canes that are divided into quadrants by twists, all on a clear strawberry-cut ground. One top facet and eight side facets. Unsigned. Edition size: 75/2 made.

STAR PATTERN

Complex canes and latticinio rods forming a star pattern on a translucent red or blue ground. One top facet and five side facets. Signed with a "P2002" cane in the base. Edition size: 75/7 made.

2002C

PURPLE BOUQUET

A bouquet of light purple flowers and buds with petals formed from millefiori canes on a black ground. Signed with a "P2002" cane in the base. Edition size: 75/9 made.

2002D

PINK CLEMATIS

A pink double clematis flower on a long stem with several leaves and two pink buds over a clear ground with a star-cut base. Signed with a "P" cane near the base of the stem. Edition size: 75/2 made.

2002E

RUBY OVERLAY

Several different colored flowers with green stems and leaves set on a white lace ground with a translucent ruby overlay. One top facet, six large and six small side facets, and fancy cutting between the side facets. Signed with a "P2002" cane in the base. Edition size: 75/2 made.

2002F

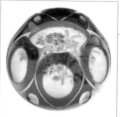

2002G

THREE-DIMENSIONAL BOUQUET
A large bouquet of blue and yellow flowers set on a black ground. One top facet and eighteen side facets. Signed with a "P" cane next to the base of the stems. Edition size: 40/1 made, plus 1 unfinished.

2002L

LITTLE GEM
An amethyst flower with two buds set on a clear ground with a strawberry-cut base. One top facet and four rows of tiny close-set notch facets extending part way down the side. Diamond-cut base. Signed with a "P" cane next to the base of the stem. Edition size: 50/1 made, plus 3 unfinished.

unfinished

2002M

LITTLE GEM
A yellow and white five-petaled flower on a stem with leaves on a translucent blue ground. One top facet and thirty side facets. Signed with a "P2002" cane in the base. Edition size: 50/1 made, plus 7 unfinished.

Christmas
Weights

SNOWMEN
Two snowmen with scarves on snow over a clear ground. The outside of the weight is frosted. One large front facet. Two small stars are cut on the rear. Scratch-signed "P" and the edition number on the base. Edition size: 250.

1997

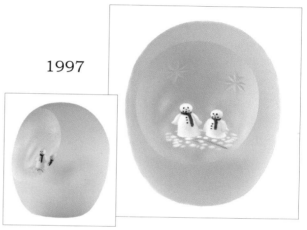

WINTER PLAYGROUND
A boy pulling a sled across a snowy field while an owl watches from a barren tree. One top facet and five side facets. Scratch-signed "P" and the edition number on the base. Edition size: 200.

1998

THREE CANDLES
Three red candles on Christmas boughs over a white lace ground. One top facet and six side facets. Signed with a "P1999" cane in the base. Edition size: 200.

1999

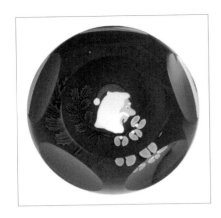

2000

SANTA CLAUS
A Santa Claus caricature set with holly and mistletoe over a translucent dark blue ground. One top facet and five side facets. Signed with a "P2000" cane and the edition number inscribed on the base. Edition size: 200.

2001

SYMBOLS OF CHRISTMAS
Holly and berries, a poinsettia flower, and golden bells set on a translucent dark blue ground. One top facet and five side facets. Signed with a "P2001" cane in the base. Edition size: 200.

Limited Edition and General Range Weights

In the descriptions of the Limited Edition and General Range Weights, the following standards are used. The Glossary contains additional definitions of the terms used.

SIZES: All sizes are approximate.
    Magnum: Diameter of more than 3-1/2 inches. Specific sizes are given.
    Large: Diameter of approximately 3 inches
    Medium: Diameter of approximately 2-1/2 inches
    Small: Diameter of approximately 2 inches
    Miniature: Diameter of less than 2 inches
    Bottles: Heights include the stopper. Diameters are given at the widest point.

COLOR VARIATIONS: Ground and cane colors vary unless a specific color is indicated. Different cane colors can cause major differences in the appearance of the weight by accenting different parts of the design.

BASES: All paperweight bases are hollow-ground unless otherwise indicated. The bases of bottles and glasses vary and are not specified.

PATTERNS: Designs are described from the center out. The number of millefiori rings and radial twists, as well as the number of canes in groups, may occasionally vary. See the next page for an enlarged photograph showing how millefiori patterns are described in this book.

Some weights were issued in both domed and faceted versions of the same design. This is indicated in the individual descriptions. The faceted version is designated by the letter "A" per the factory literature. It should be noted that Perthshire also designated some design or size changes by the letter "A" (PP2A, PP19A, PP133A, PP156A, PP178A, for example). These are treated as separate model numbers and are listed separately in the text.

For model numbers that were in production prior to the period covered in this book and remained in production after midyear 1997, the design in production during 1997 is shown for reference. Earlier design variations can be found in *The Complete Guide to Perthshire Paperweights* by Colin & Debby Mahoney and Gary & Marge McClanahan.

SIGNATURES/DATES: The standard signature of the letter "P" in a cane is referred to as a "P" cane and is undated unless stated otherwise. "Dated 'P' cane" refers to a cane containing both the letter "P" and a date showing the year in which the weight was issued. Photographs of various signature/date canes are shown in the Identification section.

2002 GENERAL RANGE WEIGHTS: The indication of General Range weights planned for 2002 was based on the fact that they were included on the 2002 factory price list. It is assumed that these weights were of the same designs that were made in 2001. Since the General Range weights are not dated, there is no way of knowing whether these weights were actually made as part of the 2002 model year.

EDITION SIZES: Edition sizes are unlimited unless stated otherwise. Limited Edition sizes vary from 250 to 400 per year. Midyear edition sizes vary from 50 to 200.

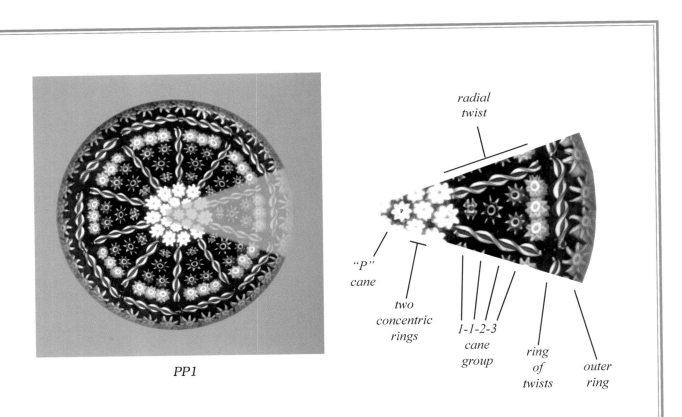

PP1

Section of a PP1 showing how the cane groups are counted. This pattern has a center "P" cane, two concentric rings of canes, and ten radial twists separating cane groups of 1-1-2-3, then a ring of twists and an outer ring of canes.

Large millefiori weight with a pattern of canes and twists. Last design change in 1982. Made 1969 – 2002.

PP1

Medium millefiori weight with a pattern of canes and twists. Last design change in 1978. Made 1969 – 2002.

PP2

Miniature millefiori weight with a center "P" cane surrounded by two rings of canes and ten radial twists separating cane groups of 1-1-2-2 on a color ground. Made 1999 – 2002.

PP2A

Miniature weight with a concentric millefiori pattern. Made 1969 – 1973 and 1984 – 1998. A few weights were made in 1983, but were not exported.

PP3

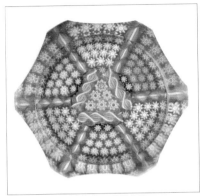

1996 – 1998

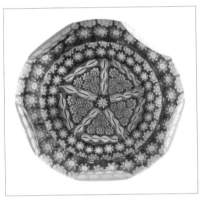

1999

PP5

Medium millefiori weight with a pattern of millefiori canes and twists. Weights made in 1999 have a center "P" cane surrounded by five short radial twists separating cane groups of 1-2-3, and dividing a ring of five twists, all surrounded by two rings of canes on a translucent color ground. Beginning in 2000, the weights have a center "P" cane surrounded by six radial twists separating cane groups of 1-2-3-4 on a color ground. Weights made in 1999 have one top facet and five side facets. Weights made after 1999 have one top facet and six side facets. Made 1969 – 2002.

2000 – 2002

PP7

Large millefiori weight with a two-layered fountain of crushed millefiori canes. Beginning in 1997, Perthshire made weights similar to the PP7 design made in 1969 – 1971, except that the weights had a black ground. These weights were designated "PP7" on invoices, but were not listed or shown in any official Perthshire literature until they appeared on the price list for 2002. Sold in 1997, 1998 and 1999.

PP18

Millefiori closepack doorknob. Made 1969 – 1978 and 1984 – 2002.

1995 – 1999

PP18A

2000 – 2002

Millefiori doorknob. Doorknobs made from 1995 to 1999 have a central millefiori cluster surrounded by five clusters, set on a blue ground, and are domed. Doorknobs made after 1999 have a closepack design with one top facet and five side facets. Made 1995 – 2002.

PP18B

Millefiori doorknob with a center "P" cane surrounded by three rings of canes, numerous short radial twists separated by single millefiori canes at their outer edge, and an outer ring of canes on a color ground. Made 2000 – 2002.

PP18C

Millefiori doorknob identical to the PP18B design, but with a single top facet. Made 2000 – 2002.

Large weight with scrambled millefiori canes on a black ground. Signed with a dated "P" cane in the base. Made 1969 – 1980 and 1987 – 2002. Limited edition.

PP19

Medium weight with scrambled millefiori canes on a black ground. Made 1995 – 2002. Signed with a dated "P" cane in the base. Limited edition.

PP19A

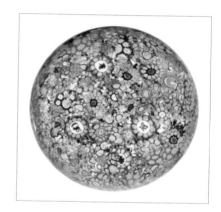

In *The Complete Guide to Perthshire Paperweights*, part of the description for a PP21 states "Perthshire literature from 1971 shows PP21 as a 'seaweed weight on seabed effect.' However, factory production records do not support this. There is no mention of a PP21 of any type in 1972. A 1971 dealer's literature shows a photo of a seaweed weight and designates it 'P9.' This is not a Perthshire number."

Although a photo of an actual seaweed weight was not available when *The Complete Guide to Perthshire Paperweights* was published, one is now.

PP21

Medium weight with a millefiori heart design. Last design change in 1997. Made 1981 – 1999.

PP46

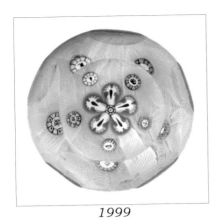

1999

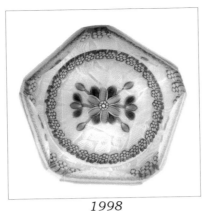

1998

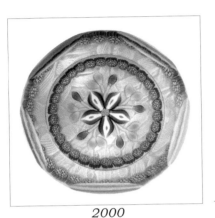

2000

PP47

2001

Medium millefiori weight with a design change each year since 1993. The 1998 design has yellow and pink flowers surrounded by a ring of pink canes on a white lace ground. Weights made in 1999 have a blue and white lampwork flower surrounded by five picture canes on a white lace ground. The 2000 weights have an amethyst and white flower with red buds and pale green leaves surrounded by a ring of blue complex canes on a white lace ground. Weights made in 2001 have a blue flower closely surrounded by three similar blue flowers and green leaves on a red/white lace ground. The 2002 design has three five-petaled blue flowers with pale green stems and leaves on a cushion of scrambled latticinio over a translucent blue ground. All are signed with a dated "P" cane in the base. The designs for 1998 – 2000 and 2002 have one top facet and five side facets, although a quantity of domed 2002 weights were marketed. The design made in 2001 has one top facet and six side facets. Made 1981 – 2002. Limited edition.

2002

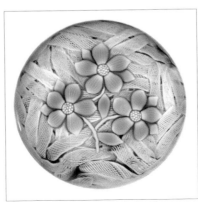

2002 Unfinished

2002 Unfinished Bottom

46

Large millefiori weight with a pattern of canes and twists the same as the PP1 design, but with one top facet and five side facets. Last design change in 1997. Made 1983 – 2002.

PP58

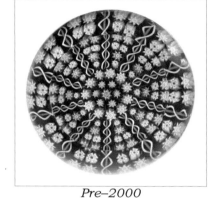

Pre–2000

Medium millefiori weight with a pattern of canes and twists the same as the PP2 design, but with faceting. Weights made prior to 2000 have one top facet. Weights made in 2000 and thereafter have one top facet and five side facets. Made 1983 – 2002.

PP59

2000 — 2002

Large millefiori weight with a pattern of canes and short radial twists. There were no changes in the basic design, although the number of radial twists varied widely. Made 1983 – 2002.

PP62

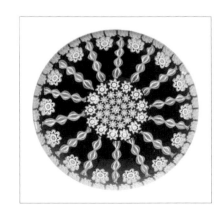

47

PP73   Doorknob with a concentric millefiori design and fluted edges. Made 1984 – 2002.

PP75   Miniature pressed weight with concentric millefiori canes and fluted edges. Made 1985 – 2002.

PP76   Small cabinet knob with concentric millefiori canes and fluted edges. Made 1985 – 2002.

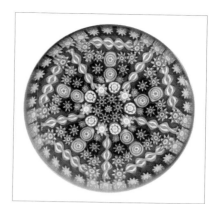

PP94

1998

Large millefiori weight with a pattern of canes and twists. Beginning in 2000, the design had a center "P" cane surrounded by three rings of pink and white canes and many radial twists separating cane groups of 1-1-1-1 on a black ground. A version with one top facet and five side facets was made in 2000 and thereafter and was designated PP94A. Made 1987 – 2002.

PP94A

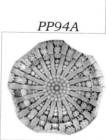

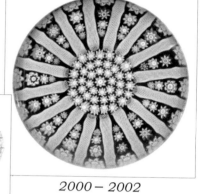

2000 – 2002

Medium millefiori weight with a center colored picture cane of a butterfly. Made 1989 – 1999.

PP108

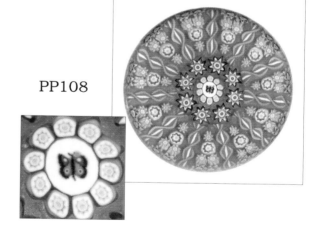

Medium millefiori weight with a star of millefiori canes. Made 1989 – 1999.

PP119

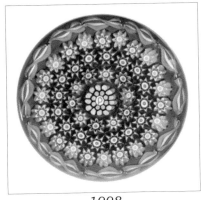

1998

PP123

Miniature millefiori weight. Weights made in 1999 and thereafter have a center "P" cane surrounded by a ring of canes, six short radial twists separating large canes, a ring of twist segments separated by pairs of canes, and an outer ring of canes on a color ground. Made 1990 – 2002.

1999

PP124

Medium millefiori weight with a pattern of canes and twists. Last design change in 1996. Made 1990 – 1999.

PP156A

Small millefiori weight with a central picture cane of a thistle surrounded by five concentric rings of simple canes. Made 1997 – 1998. Signed with a "P" cane in the base.

Small pressed millefiori weight with a concentric millefiori design. Made 1995 – 2002.

PP163

Small pressed weight with a pattern of canes and twists. Made 1996 – 2002.

PP170

Medium pressed millefiori weight with a design of canes and twists. Weights made in 1998 and thereafter have a center "P" cane surrounded by a ring of canes, nine short radial twists separating cane groups of 1-1-2, and an outer ring of canes on a color ground. Made 1996 – 2002.

PP171

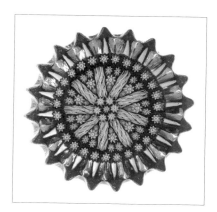

Medium millefiori closepack weight of all simple canes set on a translucent ground. Signed with a "P" cane in the center of the design. Made 1997 – 1999.

PP178

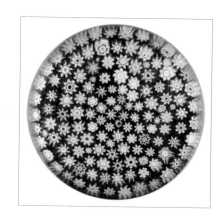

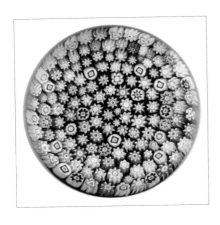

PP178A — Small millefiori closepack weight of all simple canes set on a translucent ground. Signed with a "P" cane in the center of the design. Made 1997 – 2002.

PP186 — Large weight with a Scottish thistle of millefiori canes surrounded by a ring of canes on a translucent dark blue ground. The weight has a top facet and five side facets. Signed with a "P" in the center cane or a "P" cane in the base. Made 1998 – 1999.

PP187 — Large millefiori weight with a center cane surrounded by three interlaced ovals of canes on a black or translucent blue ground. Signed with a "P" in the center cane. Made 1998 – 1999.

PP187A — Medium millefiori weight of the same design as PP187. The weight has a translucent blue ground. Made 1999 – 2002.

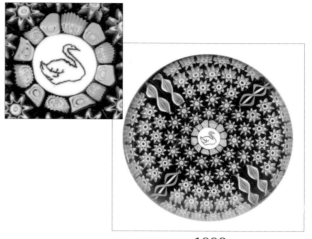

1998

Medium millefiori weight with a large center picture cane of a swan surrounded by two rings of canes. In the 1998 weight, this center design is surrounded by two short radial twists alternating with two pairs of short radial twists that separate cane groups of 4-5-6 on an opaque color ground. In 1999, the center design is surrounded by eight short radial twists that separate 2-3-3 cane groups. Signed with a "P" cane in the base. Made 1998 – 1999.

PP188

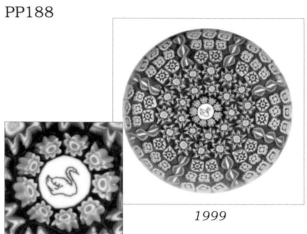

1999

Not issued.   PP189

Not issued.   PP190

Not issued.   PP191

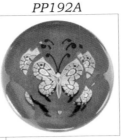

PP192A

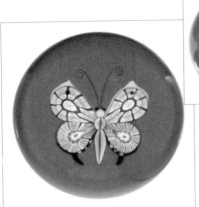

PP192

Medium weight with a lampwork butterfly with millefiori cane wings on an opaque bright red ground. Signed with a "P1998" cane in the base. A version with a top facet and six side facets is designated PP192A. Limited edition.

PP193

Medium millefiori weight with a center cane surrounded by three rings of canes, a ring of short radial twists separated by small canes, then a ring of canes and another ring of short radial twists separated by small canes, and an outer ring of canes on a translucent color ground. Signed with a "P1998" cane in the base. Limited edition.

PP194

Large millefiori weight with a large yellow five-petaled flower surrounded by a ring of canes and ten short radial twists separating cane groups of 1-2 and a short twist on a translucent ruby or blue ground. Signed with a "P1998" cane in the base. A version with a top facet and five side facets is designated PP194A. Limited edition.

PP194A

Large millefiori weight with a center complex millefiori cane surrounded by four clusters of complex millefiori canes alternating with four picture canes on a carpet of pale green canes on a translucent color ground. Signed with a "P1998" cane in the base. A version with a top facet and eight side facets is designated PP195A. Limited edition.

PP195

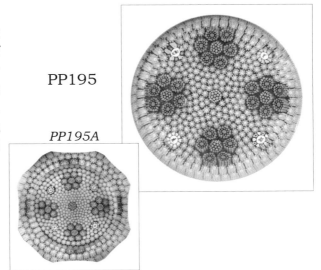

PP195A

Large millefiori weight with a five-petaled pink flower surrounded by a five-pointed star pattern outlined by a row of blue and a row of pink millefiori canes with single complex millefiori canes set between the star points on a translucent green ground. The weight has a large top facet and five side facets. Signed with a "P1998" cane in the base. Limited edition.

PP196

Large millefiori weight with a colored picture cane of a rooster surrounded by a ring of canes, seven short radial twists separating cane groups of 1-2-3-4, a ring of twist segments alternating with pairs of canes, and two outer rings of canes on a translucent green ground. Signed with a "P1998" cane in the base. A version with a top facet and seven side facets is designated PP197A. Limited edition.

PP197

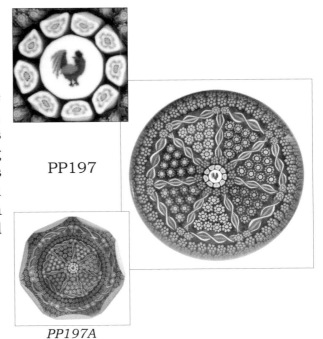

PP197A

55

PP198

Miniature millefiori weight with a complex center cane surrounded by two rings of canes, a ring of short radial latticinio rods separated by single small canes, and an outer ring of canes on a translucent color ground. Signed with a "P1998" cane in the base. Limited edition.

PP199

Medium millefiori weight with a large complex center cane surrounded by radial blue and white twists alternating with white latticinio rods on an opaque red ground. Signed with a "P" cane in the base. Made in 1999 only.

PP200

PP200A

Miniature millefiori weight with a complex center cane surrounded by a ring of canes and nine white radial latticinio rods separating cane groups of 1-1, with the outer canes being large blue/white canes, all on an opaque red ground. Signed with a "P1999" cane in the base. A version with a top facet and five side facets is designated PP200A. Limited edition.

PP201

Medium millefiori weight with a center cane surrounded by two rings of canes, eight short radial twists separating complex panels that include a short radial millefiori twist and millefiori canes, and then an outer ring of canes on a translucent color ground. Signed with a "P1999" cane in the base. Limited edition.

Medium millefiori weight with a pale blue five-petaled flower with a dark green stem and two leaves surrounded by four rings of canes on a translucent blue ground. Signed with a "P1999" cane in the base. A version with a top facet and five side facets is designated PP202A. Limited edition.

PP202

PP202A

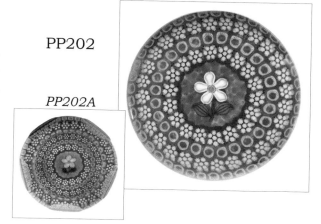

Medium millefiori weight with a complex center cane surrounded by two rings of complex canes, a ring of short radial twists alternating with large canes, and an outer ring of large canes separated by pairs of short twists on a translucent color ground. Signed with a "P1999" cane in the base. A version with a top facet and six side facets is designated PP203A. Limited edition.

PP203

PP203A

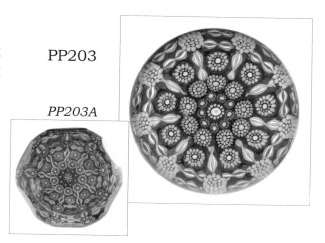

Large millefiori weight with a complex center cane surrounded by a ring of similar canes, and a complex arrangement of large and small millefiori canes and short latticinio rods, all surrounded by a ring of canes on a translucent color ground. Signed with a "P1999" cane in the base. A version with a top facet and five or six side facets is designated PP204A. Limited edition.

PP204

PP204A

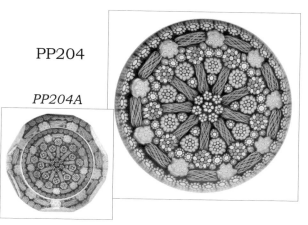

Large weight with three lampwork flowers with buds, green leaves, and stems surrounded by two rings of complex millefiori canes on a translucent green ground. The weight has a top facet and five side facets. Signed with a "P1999" cane in the base. Limited edition.

PP205

PP206

PP206A

Magnum weight with a nosegay of three large millefiori cane flowers, green leaves, and a stem surrounded by an outer complex pattern of six light-colored short radial twists and large and small canes giving the impression of a six-pointed star. The weight has a white lace ground and a diameter of 3-1/2 inches. Signed with a "P1999" cane in the base. A version with a top facet and six side facets is designated PP206A. Limited edition.

PP207

Medium millefiori weight with a group of complex canes forming a diamond shape, surrounded by parallel latticinio strips, and further surrounded by a pattern of large and small millefiori canes and an outer ring of canes on a translucent color ground. Signed with a "P1999" cane in the base. Issued midyear 1999. Limited edition.

PP208

Medium weight with a large complex center cane resting on radial twists of bold red/yellow alternating with fine twists of white, red, and yellow on a blue ground. Signed with a "P" cane in the base and the edition number inscribed on the base. Issued midyear 1999. Made in 1999 only. Limited edition.

PP209

Medium weight with a three-dimensional white flower surrounded by a ring of six white flowers alternating with teardrop petals on a translucent blue ground. The weight has a top facet and six side facets. Signed with a "P1999" cane in the base. Issued midyear 1999. Limited edition.

Large millefiori weight with a large complex center cane surrounded by a ring of canes and ten radial latticinio rods separating cane groups of 1-1-1 in graduated sizes on a translucent color ground. Signed with a "P1999" cane in the base. A version with a top facet and five side facets is designated PP210A. Issued midyear 1999. Limited edition.

PP210

PP210A

Large weight with a three-dimensional bouquet of deep-pink roses, amber flowers and blue buds with green stems and leaves on a clear ground. The weight has a top facet, twelve side facets, and a strawberry-cut base. Signed with a "P" cane at the base of the stems. Issued midyear 1999. Made in 1999 only. Limited edition.

PP211

Miniature millefiori weight with a complex center cane surrounded by a ring of complex canes, eight short radial twists alternating with cane groups of 1-1, and an outer ring of complex canes on a translucent color ground. The weight has a top facet and eight side facets. Signed with a "P2000" cane in the base. Limited edition.

PP212

PP213A

Medium millefiori weight with a center cane surrounded by two rings of canes, a ring of six short radial latticinio rods alternating with pairs of canes, then six short radial latticinio rods separating cane groups of 4-4-5, and an outer ring of canes on a translucent color ground. Signed with a "P2000" cane in the base. A version with a top facet and six side facets is designated PP213A. Limited edition.

PP213

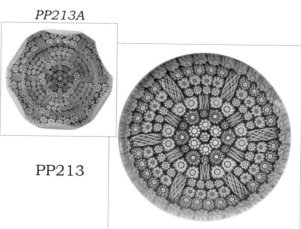

PP214

Medium millefiori weight with a large complex center cane surrounded by a square pattern of white latticinio rods and canes on a translucent color ground. The weight has a top facet and four large oval side facets. Signed with a "P2000" cane in the base. Limited edition.

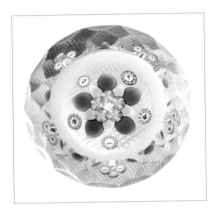

PP215

Medium millefiori weight with a center flower of a millefiori cane group in the center and lampwork petals of varying colors surrounded by five picture canes on a clear ground. The weight has a top facet, sixty side facets, and a grid-cut base. Scratch-signed "P" on the base. Made in 2000 only. Limited edition.

PP216

PP216A

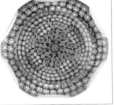

Large millefiori weight with a large complex center cane surrounded by a complex pattern of twists and canes forming a cross surrounded by two outer rings of canes on a translucent color ground. Signed with a "P2000" cane in the base. A version with a top facet and six side facets is designated PP216A. Limited edition.

PP217

Large millefiori weight with a center cane surrounded by a group of four large complex canes, a ring of four medium complex canes alternating with groups of four smaller canes, then a complex pattern of short radial twists and canes, all surrounded by two outer rings of canes. The weight has a translucent color ground, a top facet, and sixteen side facets. Signed with a "P2000" cane in the base. Limited edition.

Large weight with a large blue lampwork flower with buds, stems, and leaves surrounded by a diamond-shaped pattern of pale green rods and four smaller blue flowers on a black ground. The weight has a top facet and eight side facets. Signed with a "P2000" cane in the base and the edition number inscribed on the base. Limited edition.

PP218

Large weight with a turquoise and white lampwork flower with green leaves set within a seven-pointed star of three rows of millefiori canes with short radial twists forming the star points. A turquoise bud with a green stem and leaf is set between each pair of star points. The weight has a translucent amethyst-red ground, a top facet and seven side facets. Signed with a "P2000" cane in the base. Limited edition.

PP219

Miniature millefiori closepack of complex canes on a translucent blue ground. Signed with a "P2000" cane in the base and an inscribed "P" on the base. Issued midyear 2000. Limited edition.

PP220

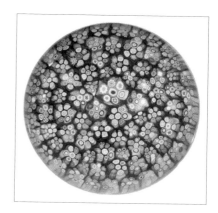

Small weight with a lampwork bouquet of amethyst and yellow flowers with deep green stems and leaves on a clear ground. The weight has a top facet, six side facets, and a frosted ring on the base. Signed with an inscribed "P" and the edition number on the basal ring. Issued midyear 2000. Made in 2000 only. Limited edition.

PP221

PP222

Medium weight with a central flower with four pink millefiori cane petals, a bud, green stem and leaves surrounded by a hexagon of twists with a millefiori cane at each corner and an outer ring of canes on a translucent blue ground. The weight has a top facet and six side facets. Signed with a "P2000" cane in the base. Issued midyear 2000. Limited edition.

PP223

Medium weight with two pink and two green lampwork flowers with multicolored tendrils on a translucent green ground. The weight has a top facet and eight side facets. Signed with a "P2000" cane in the base. Issued midyear 2000. Limited edition.

PP224

Large weight with a central dark blue lampwork flower with yellow stamens and green leaves surrounded by eight complex canes that are set between pairs of radial twists on a yellow lace ground. The weight has a top facet and eight side facets. Signed with a "P2000" cane in the base. Issued midyear 2000. Limited edition.

PP225

Large weight with a three-dimensional bouquet of two pink flowers, four red buds, green stems and leaves on a clear ground. The weight has a top facet, five large oval side facets, and a grid-cut base. Signed with a "P" cane near the base of the stems and scratch-signed with a "P" and the edition number on the base. Issued midyear 2000. Made in 2000 only.

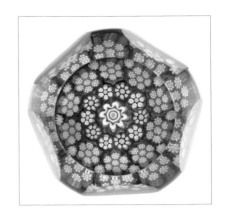

Miniature weight with a large center cane surrounded by a ring of small canes and a ring of large canes alternating with small canes on a translucent color ground. The weight has a top facet and five side facets. Signed with a "P2001" cane in the base. Limited edition.

PP226

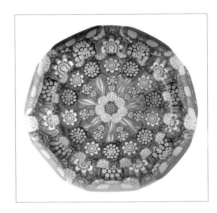

Medium millefiori weight with a complex center cane surrounded by a ring of canes, a ring of short radial twists separating cane groups of 1-1, and two additional rings of canes on a translucent color ground. The weight has a top facet and seven side facets. Signed with a "P2001" cane in the base. Limited edition.

PP227

Medium millefiori weight with a large complex center cane surrounded by a ring of canes, a ring of nine short radial twists alternating with single canes, another ring of canes, and then nine additional short twists that separate groups of two canes and an outer twist on a translucent color ground. Signed with a "P2001" cane in the base. A version with a top facet and six side facets is designated PP228A. Limited edition.

PP228

PP228A

Large millefiori weight with a square pattern with twenty-five closepacked canes in the center surrounded by squares of orange latticinio rods alternating with squares of millefiori canes with a large complex cane at each corner. The weight has a translucent color ground, a top facet and four side facets. Signed with a "P2001" cane in the base. Limited edition.

PP229

PP230

Large weight with a five-petaled ruby flower surrounded by a five-sided design formed by blue rods in the form of arches, with each arch framing a nosegay of millefiori buds and a large green leaf. The weight has a white lace ground, a top facet, and five side facets. Signed with a "P2001" cane in the base. Limited edition.

PP231

PP228A

Large millefiori weight with a complex center cane surrounded by a ring of canes, a hexagon of canes, a hexagon of six latticinio rods alternating with pairs of canes, another ring of canes, and six short radial latticinio rods extending through three outer hexagons of latticinio rods and canes on a translucent color ground. Signed with a "P2001" cane in the base. A version with a top facet and six side facets is designated PP231A. Limited edition.

PP232

Medium weight with a large white lampwork flower with a millefiori cane center topping a crown of white latticinio rods alternating with twists of amethyst, white, and blue set on a pale blue core. Signed with a "P2001" cane in the base. Limited edition.

PP233

Medium weight with a large red stylized flower with green leaves set at the center of orange radial spokes on a translucent blue ground. Signed with a "P2001" cane in the base. Limited edition.

Small weight with a large complex cane surrounded by two rings of canes, and a ring of large pale blue/white canes on a black ground. Signed with a "P2001" cane in the base. Issued midyear 2001. Limited edition.

PP234

Large weight with a center picture cane of a dog surrounded by six rings of canes and an outer ring of hollow white latticinio rods pulled down to form a basket. Signed with a "P2001" cane in the base. Issued midyear 2001. Limited edition.

PP235

Small weight with a blue lampwork flower surrounded by three ruby buds with green leaves alternating with three pairs of amber buds on a white lace ground. The weight has a top facet and three side facets. Signed with a "P2001" cane in the base. Issued midyear 2001. Limited edition.

PP236

PP237A

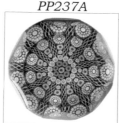

Large millefiori weight with a complex center cane surrounded by two rings of canes and many short white radial latticinio rods separating cane groups of 1-1-1 that include a large pink/white cane at the outer edge, all on a black ground. Signed with a "P2001" cane in the base. A version with a top facet and six side facets is designated PP237A. Issued midyear 2001. Limited edition.

PP237

65

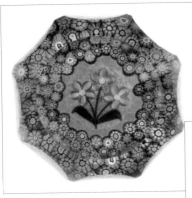

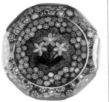

PP238

Magnum weight with one pink, one amber, and one blue flower with dark green leaves surrounded by a border of randomly scattered millefiori canes on a translucent ruby or blue ground. The weight has a top facet and eight side facets. Signed with a "P2001" cane in the base. Issued midyear 2001. Limited edition.

PP239

Tall weight of unusual shape with a three-dimensional blue and ivory flower with yellow stamens surrounded by small blue and ruby buds over three large green leaves on a black ground. The weight has a top facet with scalloped edges, small flutes around the edge of the ground, and eight facets near the base. Signed with an inscribed "P" and the edition number on the base. Issued midyear 2001. Made in 2001 only. Limited edition.

PP240

Medium weight with a bouquet of dark blue flowers with yellow stamens set on light green leaves on a clear ground. The weight has a top facet, six side facets, and a feather-cut base. Signed with a "P" cane at base of stems and/or with an inscribed "P" and edition number near the base. Issued midyear 2001. Made in 2001 only. Limited edition.

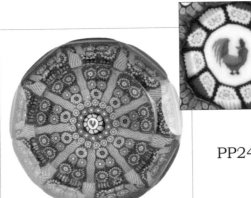

PP241

Medium weight with a colored picture cane of a rooster surrounded by two rings of canes and nine short radial latticinio rods separating cane groups of 1-2-2 on a translucent color ground. The weight has a top facet and nine side facets. Signed with a "P2001" cane in the base. Issued as part of the 2001 Christmas Collection. Limited edition.

The following "PP" numbers were never officially released.

Medium millefiori weight with a center cane surrounded by two rings of canes, eight short radial twists with a single large cane at the outer ends separating groups of 1-2-2-2 white stardust canes on a colored ground. Signed with a "P" cane in the center of the design. Planned for 2002.

PP242

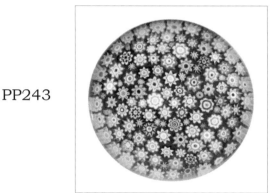

Large millefiori weight with closepacked simple millefiori canes on an opaque bright red ground. Signed with a "P" cane in the setup. Originally issued as part of the 2001 Christmas Collection, where it was called "Big and Bright." Planned as PP243 in 2002.

PP243

Small millefiori weight with closepacked simple millefiori canes on an opaque bright red ground. Signed with a "P" cane in the setup. It was sold by several UK dealers under the names "Small and Bright" and "Star Bright." The design was called "Red Scrambled" in the 2001 catalogue and was planned to be called PP243A in the 2002 catalogue. Made in 2001 and planned to be made in 2002.

PP243A

Medium millefiori weight with a large complex center cane surrounded by two rings of canes, twelve short latticinio rods alternating with cane groups of 1-1, a ring of short latticinio rods alternating with single canes, and an outer ring of canes on a translucent color ground. Signed with a "P2002" cane in the base. A version with a top facet and six side facets is designated PP244A. Planned to be a limited edition. Finished – 53; unfinished – 7.

PP244A

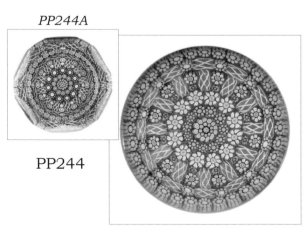

PP244

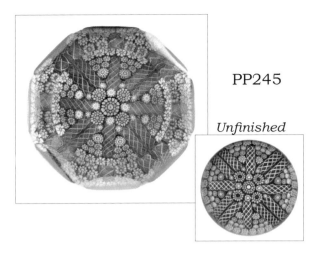

PP245

Unfinished

Medium millefiori weight with a complex center cane surrounded by four large canes separated by four small canes and a complex pattern of radial latticinio rods and millefiori canes forming a double cross on a translucent color ground. The weight has a top facet and eight side facets. Some unfinished domed weights were sold. Signed with a "P2002" cane in the base. Planned to be a limited edition. Finished – 22; unfinished – 20.

PP246

Medium weight with a blue flower and bud on a green stem with leaves on a doily of white millefiori canes surrounded by a ring of white and blue canes and an outer ring of blue and white canes pulled down to form a blue basket. The weight has an opaque red ground and a top facet. Signed with a "P2002" cane in the base. Planned to be a limited edition. Finished – 4

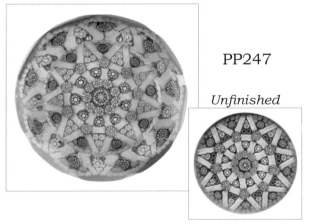

PP247

Unfinished

Large millefiori weight with a large center cane surrounded by a ring of canes and a complex pattern of short latticinio rods and millefiori canes on a translucent color ground. The weight has a top facet and nine side facets. Some unfinished domed weights were sold. Signed with a "P2002" cane in the base. Planned to be a limited edition. Finished – 16; unfinished – 21

PP248

Large millefiori weight with a center cane surrounded by a concentric pattern of large and small millefiori canes set around large blue and green canes on a translucent amethyst ground. Signed with a "P2002" cane in the base. Planned to be a limited edition. Finished – 41; unfinished – 1.

Large millefiori weight with a hexagonal pattern formed by six hexagons of canes outlined by latticinio rods on a black ground. The weight has a hexagonal top facet with a ring of touching side facets. Signed with a "P2002" cane in the base. Planned to be a limited edition. Finished – 16.

PP249

Special Editions

Dated

NEIL AND MIRIAM DRYSDALE WEDDING
A diamond-shaped pattern of millefiori canes with one large complex cane in the center of the diamond. Twists separate the sides of the diamond from a ring of blue canes, then a ring of sets of three pink canes alternating with three green canes. Plaques at the top and bottom of the diamond read "28•2•80" and "ND • MCL". No signature cane. Edition size is not known.

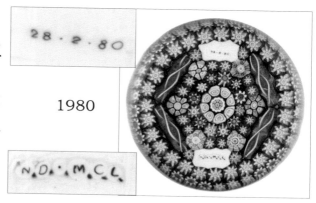

1980

PRINCESS DIANA COMMEMORATIVE
Four pale blue forget-me-nots and buds. "Diana" and "1961 ~ 1997" in yellow script, all on a translucent blue ground. One top facet and five side facets. Signed with a "P" cane in the base. Edition size: 100

1997

1997 MIDYEAR EDITION
A large weight containing a variety of complex canes on a black ground. Domed or with one top facet and six side facets. Signed with a "PP1997" cane within the design. Edition size: 50/50 made.

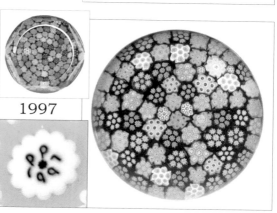

1997

71

1997

GALA 97
A miniature pressed concentric millefiori weight that is similar in design to PP75 weights, except for a "GALA 97" cane in the center. Made for the GALA '97 Conference on Language Acquisition in Edinburgh.

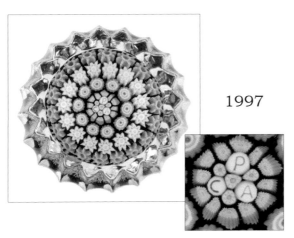

1997

PAPERWEIGHT COLLECTORS ASSOCIATION INC. (PCA) 1997 TABLE FAVOR
A miniature pressed concentric millefiori weight that is similar in design to PP75 weights, except for a "PCA" cane in the center. Signed with a dated "P" cane in the base. Approximately 500 were made.

1998

1998 MIDYEAR EDITION
A large blue flower surrounded by stems with many leaves and buds set on a white latticinio ground. One top facet and five side facets. Signed with a "P1998" cane in the base. Edition size: 50

1999

OKLAHOMA PCA
A small pressed weight with a patterned millefiori design on a translucent blue ground. The design is identical to the PP170 design except for a "PCA OK" center cane. Inscribed "1989 1999" and signed with a "P" cane in the base. Made in 1999 to commemorate the 10th anniversary of the Oklahoma PCA. Approximately 75 were made.

1999

NEIL & JANE DRYSDALE WEDDING
Similar in design to the PP94A which was issued in 2000 and thereafter. Has a flat bottom which is unusual for Perthshire weights. Scratch-signed on the bottom "Neil - Jane" and "5•11•99". The edition size is not known.

MARDI GRAS 1999
A swirl of green, yellow and purple rods over a translucent blue core topped with a large complex center cane. Inscribed "Mardi Gras 1999 NOLA" and the edition number. Signed with a "P" cane in base. Made exclusively for Lord Jim, a New Orleans, Louisiana gift shop, to commemorate the 1999 Mardi Gras. Edition size: 100.

1999

MILLENNIUM
A six-petaled ruby and white flower on yellow lace is surrounded by a ring of ruby/white canes. An outer ring of spaced canes including a "2000" cane and five colored picture canes are set on a white lace ground. Signed with a "P" cane in the base. Made in 1999 and 2000 for the Millennium. Edition size: 500.

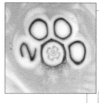

2000

2000

MARDI GRAS 2000
A three-layer "fountain" weight with a layer of crushed lavender and white canes above a layer of crushed yellow and white canes, with the four corners and the center of each layer pulled down to meet a cushion of crushed green and white canes on a black ground. Similar in design to PP8 "Aladdin's Cave" weights except for colors of the canes and ground. Inscribed "New Orleans Mardi Gras 2000" and "Perthshire" with the edition number. Made exclusively for Lord Jim to commemorate the 2000 Mardi Gras. Edition size: 50.

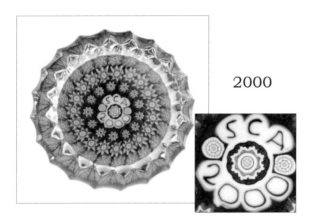

2000

MINIATURE CONCENTRIC MILLEFIORI
A miniature pressed concentric millefiori weight that is similar in design to PP75 weights, except for a "SCA 2000" center cane. Made in 2000 exclusively for Steve Cole Antiques of Temecula, California.

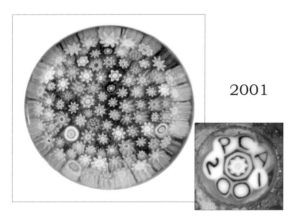

2001

PAPERWEIGHT COLLECTORS ASSOCIATION INC. (PCA) 2001 TABLE FAVOR
A miniature closepack of simple millefiori canes including a "P" cane on a translucent blue ground. The weight has a "PCA 2001" cane in the base. Made as table favors for attendees of the Paperweight Collectors Association Inc. convention held in Corning, New York, in May, 2001.

2001

PAPERWEIGHT COLLECTORS ASSOCIATION INC. (PCA) 2001
Two pale orange flowers and three orange buds with green stems and leaves on a translucent dark blue ground. One top facet and six side facets. Signed with a "P" cane and a "PCA 2001" cane in the base. Made exclusively for the Paperweight Collectors Association Inc.

MARDI GRAS 2001

Center "P" cane surrounded by two rings of canes and thirteen radial yellow latticinio tubes separated by single purple and white canes at their outer edges, all on a mottled green ground. Inscribed "New Orleans Mardi Gras 2001" and the edition number. Made exclusively for Lord Jim to commemorate the 2001 Mardi Gras. Edition size: 50.

2001

Undated

CRIEFF VISITOR CENTRE

The Crieff Visitor Centre consisted of Perthshire Paperweights Limited, a restaurant and a pottery factory. Visitors to the Perthshire Paperweights gift shop could purchase this weight (and many others) as a souvenir of their visit. This weight was not sold outside of the gift shop.

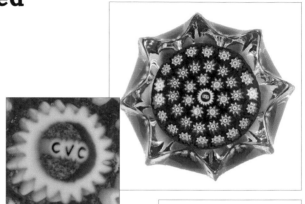

PYRAMID

A small cone-shaped pressed weight containing whole and broken canes pieces with an opaque core of red, blue, or black. These weights have a fire-polished base and are unsigned. Weights of this type were marketed in the United Kingdom in 2000 and 2001, but were not listed in Perthshire sales literature until the planned 2002 catalogue.

YELLOW-HEADED BLACKBIRD

A large weight with a North American yellow-headed blackbird perched in a clump of reeds on a clear ground. Signed with a "P" cane at the base of the reeds. Made in 2001. Edition size: 15/15 made.

BIG AND BRIGHT

A large closepack of simple canes set on an opaque red ground. Signed with a "P" cane in the setup. Issued originally as part of the 2001 Christmas Collection, the design was called PP243 in the 2002 catalogue.

RED SCRAMBLED

A small closepack of simple canes set on an opaque red ground. Signed with a "P" cane in the setup. It was sold by several UK dealers under the names "Small and Bright" and "Star Bright." The design was called PP243A in the 2002 catalogue.

PASTEL CROWN

A crown with purple/green/white twists alternating with white latticinio rods topped with a complex cane. Signed with a "P" cane in the base. Made exclusively for G.W. McClanahan in 1997. Edition size: 25/16 made.

MAGNUM BUTTERFLIES

A central butterfly with millefiori cane wings surrounded by seven similar butterflies of various colors all on a black ground. Signed with a "P" cane in the base. Made exclusively for G.W. McClanahan in 1998 and 1999. Edition size: 25/11 made.

KISSING FISH

A kissing fish with a bright pink body and green latticinio tail and fins surrounded by a hexagon of millefiori canes, a hexagon of short twists alternating with three-cane groups, and an outer ring of canes on an opaque teal ground. Signed with a "P" cane in the base. Made exclusively for L.H. Selman Ltd. Edition size: 100.

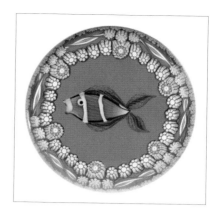

"WHISKERS"

Black and white cat surrounded by a ring of pale blue canes, a ring of twists, and a ring of pink canes on an opaque teal ground. Signed with a "P" cane in the base. Made exclusively for L.H. Selman Ltd. Edition size: 100.

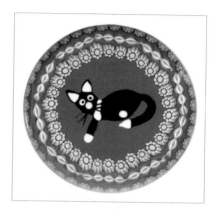

TARTAN CROWN

Five pairs of red and blue twists are separated by five pairs of white latticinio rods, all set into a pale green ground. Topped with a six-petaled blue flower with a complex center cane. Signed with a "P" cane in the base. Made exclusively for L.H. Selman Ltd. Edition size: 50.

GOLD TARTAN CROWN

Five pairs of red and blue twists are separated by five pairs of white latticinio rods, all set into a pale green ground. Topped with a six-petaled yellow flower with a complex center cane. Signed with a "P" cane in the base. Made exclusively for L.H. Selman Ltd. Edition size: 50.

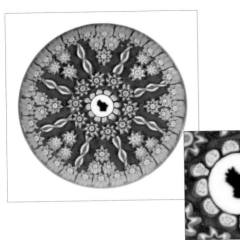

WISCONSIN 1

A miniature weight with a center silhouette cane representing the state of Wisconsin surrounded by a ring of pale blue canes and eight short radial twists separating 1-2 cane groups and then an outer ring of pink canes on an opaque teal ground. Signed with a "P" cane in the base. Made exclusively for the Bergstrom–Mahler Museum in 1998.

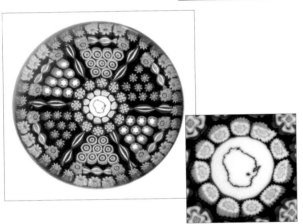

WISCONSIN 2

Small weight with a center black and white picture cane showing an outline of the state of Wisconsin surrounded by a ring of canes, six radial twists separating panels of millefiori canes with a short twist in each panel, and an outer ring of canes on a black ground. A tiny star indicates the location of the Bergstrom-Mahler Museum. Signed with a "P" cane in the base and also scratch-signed "ND PMcD" for Neil Drysdale and Peter McDougall. Made exclusively for the Bergstrom–Mahler Museum in 1999.

COUNCIL TREE 4

A large colored picture cane of a tree surrounded by a ring of canes, then ten twists separating cane groups of 1-1-2-3, and finally an outer ring of canes, all on a translucent blue ground. Cane colors vary. Signed with a "P" cane in the base. Made exclusively for the Bergstrom–Mahler Museum in 2000.

WOOD VIOLETS

White wood violets with dark green stems and leaves on a clear ground. One top facet, six large side facets, and groove cutting at the edge of the base. Signed with a "P" cane and a "BMM" cane at the base of the stems. This is the only use of this special "BMM" cane. Made exclusively for the Bergstrom–Mahler Museum in 2001. Edition size: 15/15 made.

MILLEFIORI CLOSEPACK IN BASKET

A closepack millefiori design with canes of various colors and sizes bordered with a ring of blue and ruby canes drawn down to form a stave basket. Signed with an "SG" cane in the pattern and a "P" cane in the base. Made exclusively for the Stone Gallery in England. Edition size: 50.

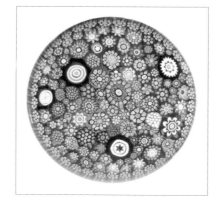

BLUE FLOWER AND MILLEFIORI

A blue flower with a complex millefiori cane center and a green stem with leaves surrounded by an arrangement of short twists and canes on a black ground. The cane in the center of the flower includes "S" and "G" canes. One top facet and five side facets. Signed with a "P" cane in the base and scratch-signed with the edition number. Made exclusively for the Stone Gallery in England in 1998 and 1999. Edition size: 25.

NEW ENGLAND PCA (NEPCA)

There are two versions. The first is domed and has a gold-colored glass transfer of the NEPCA logo surrounded by a ring of alternating twists and cane pairs, then three rings of canes on a black ground. The second has one top facet and a red glass transfer surrounded by a ring of alternating twists and cane pairs, then two rings of canes on a white lace ground. The edition sizes are unknown.

(NOTE: A glass transfer is a decal which is fired onto a glass disk.)

MINIATURE PICTURE CANE WEIGHT
A small weight with more than 20 picture canes set on a crushed millefiori ground. Limited to 25 pieces for the year 2001. Each weight came with a numbered certificate signed by Neil Drysdale.

PERTHSHIRE STAFF WEIGHT
A large blue double clematis with cupped petals and a yellow millefiori cane center on a stem with dark green leaves on a clear ground. The base has a sixty-four point star-cut. The certificate, which is dated December, 2001 and is signed "S. Drysdale," states in part, "This edition was made exclusively for the Perthshire staff in recognition of their loyal service and is limited to only seventeen pieces."

ADAM & COMPANY
A central logo cane surrounded by two rings of canes and nine radial twists separating 2-2-2 twist cane groups. One top facet and eight side facets. Made exclusively for Adam & Company in Scotland. The edition size is not known.

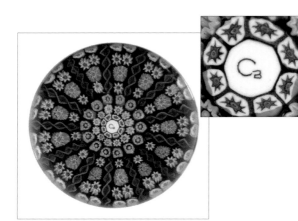

CLYDESDALE BANK
A large patterned millefiori weight with a design similar to that of early (pre-1978) PP1 weights. The design has a central logo cane surrounded by two rings of canes and thirteen radial twists separating 1-1-2-2 cane groups on a translucent dark blue ground. Made exclusively for the Clydesdale Bank International in Scotland.

GAVEL

A medium patterned millefiori weight with a design similar to that of PP2 weights. The weight has a gavel center cane surrounded by a ring of canes and eleven radial twists that separate 1-1-2-2 cane groups on a dark ground. This is believed to have been made for Sotheby's of London in the early 1970's. The edition size is believed to be between 50 and 100.

GLENFIDDICH STAG DEER

A glass transfer of a stag deer over a black ground surrounded by three rings of millefiori canes. The stag deer is the logo of the Glenfiddich Distillery in Scotland. One top facet. Signed with a "P" cane in the base. Approximately 6 were made.

SHAMROCK

A medium patterned millefiori weight with a design similar to that of PP2 weights. The weight has a shamrock center cane surrounded by a ring of canes and ten radial twists that separate 1-1-2-2 cane groups on a blue ground. Signed with a "P" cane in the base. Made for a company in Cork, Ireland.

SWISS BANK

A closepack millefiori design with two special canes. In 1998 the Swiss Bank Corporation merged with the Union Bank of Switzerland creating UBS, the largest bank in Europe. Other banks had merged with those two prior to 1998 and by adding up the years of service of all the banks, the total is a little more than 500 years of service.

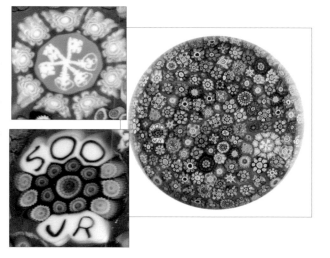

TEDDY BEAR

A lampwork teddy bear with hat and scarf surrounded by a ring of red canes and a ring of green and white canes on a white lace ground. Signed with a "P" cane in the base and inscribed with the year of manufacture on the base. Made exclusively for Harrods in England from 1986 to 1988. Edition size: 50.

CRIEFF GAS COMPANY

A PP2 design with a special central picture cane with the gas company logo. Edition size is not known.

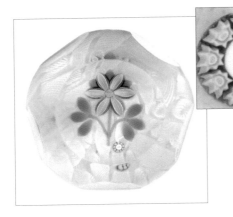

YELVERTON PAPERWEIGHT CENTRE

A pink flower on a green stem with leaves set on white lace. One top facet and five side facets. Signed with a "YPC" cane near the flower stem and a "P" cane in the base. The weight was made exclusively for the Yelverton Paperweight Centre (YPC) in England. Edition size: 100

TRIPLE OVERLAY ENCASED TRIPLE OVERLAY

A complex bouquet with several flowers of different colors, buds, leaves and stems set on an opaque blue ground inside a triple overlay of light blue over white over garnet red which is encased in clear within another triple overlay of the same colors. Only 5 were made and the overlay cutting and the bouquet varies in each one. Made in 1994.

One-of-a-Kind Weights

Bouquet on amethyst cushion with a double overlay of purple over white. "P1999" cane in the base.

Bouquet on blue cushion with a double overlay of green over white, on a pedestal. Scratch-signed "PMcD".

Dragonfly over flowers and leaves on an opaque purple ground.

Upright flower and leaves over blue cushion in an encased double overlay of red over white. "P1978" cane in the base.

Bouquet on a translucent purple ground with fancy cutting all over. "P" cane by the stems.

Bouquet on a blue ground in an encased double overlay of amethyst over white. Scratch-signed "PMcD 1-OFF".

Two pink bells hang from a
ring with green leaves, all set
on a ground of red and white
latticinio pieces.

Bouquet with a twist torsade
on a black ground. "P" cane
near the stems.

Green, blue and twist swirl
weight with a "P" cane in base.

Flower and bud on a blue
cushion in an encased
double overlay of olive over
white. "P1979" cane in the
base.

Patterned millefiori with duck
picture cane on a translucent
red ground. "P1997" cane in
the base.

Crown with blue/green twists
and white latticinio. "P" cane
in base. (circa 1992)

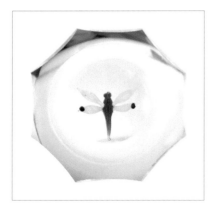

Dragonfly in clear crystal.
(circa 1970)

Square millefiori cane pattern
on white lace. "P1992" cane
in the base.

Bouquet (similar to 1982F) in
clear crystal. "P" cane at the
bottom of the bouquet.
(circa 1982)

Scattered complex canes
and picture canes with white
latticinio on a ruby ground.
"P1969" canes in the design.

Closepack design with
an outer ring of yellow
canes pulled down to
form a pedestal.

Bouquet on a red cushion in
a double overlay of blue over
white. "PMcD" cane in base.

A double overlay (of blue
over white) hollow weight
containing a penguin. "P"
cane in the base.

Encased double overlay of
red over white with a central
golliwog cane. "P1982" cane
in the base.

Patterned millefiori with
aventurine twists on an
opaque green cushion.

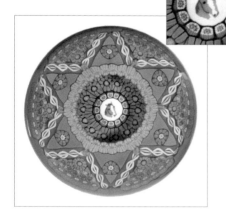

Magnum two-layered weight
with a horse-head picture
cane with concentric millefiori
on the lower layer and a
patterned millefiori top layer.
"P1983" cane in the base.

Three-flower bouquet resting
on gold-colored latticinio over
blue.

Five complex canes around
a center cane with a garland
on a clear ground.

Gecko on a tree branch with several flowers and leaves. "P" cane below the branch.

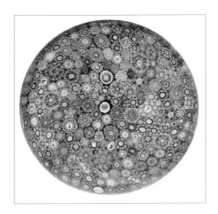

Super-magnum closepack with very complex canes. "P1991" and "PMcD" canes in the design.

Magnum weight with triangular panels.

Pansy and leaves on a clear ground.

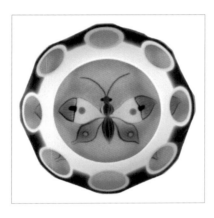

Butterfly in a triple overlay of purple over white over yellow.

Large flower and leaves surrounded by a garland on a clear ground.

Miniature patterned millefiori on clear with a star-cut base. One top facet and six side facets.

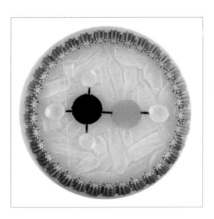

Chemical symbol for methanol. "P1981" cane in the base.

Spider web on a translucent green ground with a central "spider" cane. "P1995" cane in the base.

Upright dahlia and leaves in a triple overlay of blue over white over red.

Dragonfly hovering over a flower and bud in a single overlay encased double overlay of green over white.

Top view of the weight on the left.

Black and yellow radial twists on a black cushion ground with a complex cane at the center.

Flower with millefiori petals set on a swirl ground.

Pansy with overall honeycomb facets.

Pink and blue flower bouquet over a gold aventurine spatter ground.

Hollow weight containing a Clydesdale colt.

Closeup of the Clydesdale colt on the left.

A bouquet in a fancy cut double overlay of purple over white.

An upright two-layer flower in an encased double overlay of green over white. "P" cane in the center of the upper flower.

A smaller version of the 1970B flash overlay.

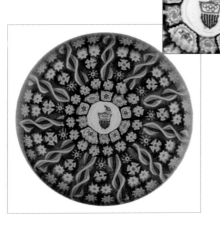

Olympic torch picture cane in a pattern similar to a PP1.

Scrambled marble containing many very complex canes and picture canes. Diameter: 1-7/8 inches.

A concentric millefiori mushroom with a center robin cane within a pink flash overlay encased double overlay of green over white. "P1978" cane in the base.

A central picture cane of a skier surrounded by four sets of holly leaves all on a white lace ground. "P1978" cane in the base.

A Santa Claus caricature set with a red flower and holly leaves all on a translucent blue ground.

Pan-Am logo weight.

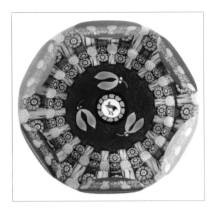

A design prototype of the
1995 Christmas weight.

Magnum bouquet of twelve
pink flowers and eighteen
buds on a clear ground. "P"
cane near the stem base.
Diameter: 4-1/2 inches.

A pink flower within a ring of
canes encircled by five nosegays, all on a yellow lace
ground.

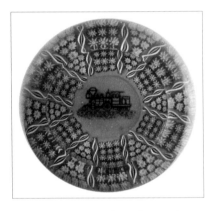

Glass transfer of a train
engine surrounded by a cane
and twist pattern set on a
blue ground.

Bouquet of blue and pink roses
and buds in clear crystal. "P"
cane below the stem.

Sulphide of a woman in a
concentric design on a black
ground.

Perthshire logo weight.

Magnum devil's fire with-
in an optic bubble sur-
round. Five inches high.
"P" cane in the base.

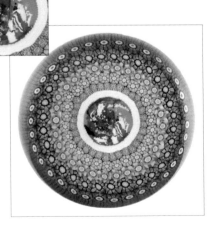

Large weight with an oasis
picture cane at the center of a
concentric design.

Blue Jay

Eight one-off weights featuring different birds of North America. All have a clear ground and a "P" cane in the design. Made for the 2001 PCA Convention Artists' Exhibit.

Cassin's Finch

Golden Kinglet

Loggerhead Shrike

Scarlet Tanager

Western Kingbird

Yellow-Billed Cuckoo

Yellow Throat

Related Items

TAZZA
A base similar to a PP22 bottle with the top flared out and a ribbon of translucent blue added.

PIN DISH
Pin dishes can be found with various base designs.

PLAQUE
A clear plaque approximately 4-3/4 inches long, 1-5/8 inches wide and ½ inch thick. Plaques were made with various lampwork and millefiori designs and cuttings.

BOTTLE
A bottle with a teardrop-shaped body and rounded stopper. Matching millefiori designs in the stopper and bottle bottom. Appears to be an early version (pre-1980) of the PP42 bottle with a concentric millefiori stopper instead of the later elongated stoppers with spiral twists. The pre-1980 literature does not reference this as an issued design.

SHADOW BOXES
Shadow boxes (one inch magnifying plastic boxes) listed in the 1999 through 2001 catalogues. These contain simple and complex canes, twists and picture canes.

CREAMER

The PP23 Cream Jug was made from 1973 through 1975. The issued design was approximately 4-1/2 inches high and 2-3/4 inches in diameter. This appears to be a design prototype that is lower (2-1/2 inches high) and wider (3-1/4 inches in diameter) than the design that was issued.

SUGAR BOWL

The PP29 Sugar Bowl was made only in 1975. It had a concentric millefiori design in the base and straight sides that slope outward bottom to top. This prototype also has the concentric millefiori base but has more rounded bowl-shaped curving sides and a flared top rim.

FANCY VASE

Perthshire made fancy vases with various shapes and designs. This tall tulip vase incorporates the shaded color motif reminiscent of Monart Glass pieces (see page 98 for similar colored pieces from Perthshire) coupled with a paperweight base including Perthshire picture canes.

PAPERWEIGHT VASE
A tall (6 inches) clear flared vase with a paperweight base in the style of the classic antique pieces from St. Louis and Baccarat. The base for this vase is a PP2 paperweight.

DOUBLE OVERLAY BOWL
Perthshire made bowls in various shapes and designs. This bowl has a double overlay of green over white shading to a green flash overlay towards the top. Eight large side facets and eight smaller side facets. Base contains one large central complex cane surrounded by three rings of canes.

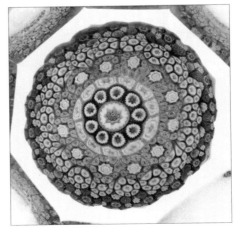

PEDESTAL
Perthshire made pedestals with various paper-weight designs. This is a variation of the 1977A paperweight with a pedestal and clear foot.

RING HOLDER
Ring holders can be found with many different paperweight bases. This one is 7 inches tall and has a crown base.

TIE TACK
Sections of millefiori canes or picture canes have a small dome of clear glass applied to one side and the pin hardware applied to the back.

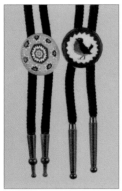 

BOLO TIE CLASP
Large sections of millefiori canes or picture canes have a small dome of clear glass applied to one side and the clasp hardware applied to the back.

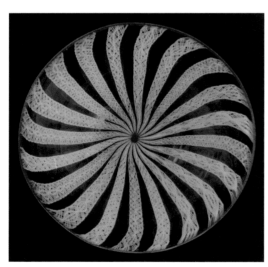

FANCY BOWL
Perthshire made fancy bowls with or without paperweight bases. This bowl has 20 latticinio rods and a translucent red base.

MILLEFIORI TOOL SET WHIMSY
A scrambled millefiori design covers the surface of a glass hammer and screwdriver. This set is part of the permanent collection of the Bergstrom–Mahler Museum of Glass.

SWAN
This swan's base is the same design and setup as a PP66. Clear crystal surrounding the base has been sculpted into a swan.

Around 1992 Perthshire began producing a line of glassware with colors fashioned after the Monart Art Glass line that was made by the Ysart family at John Moncrieff Ltd. between 1924 and 1961. Vasart and Strathearn also made similar items during their production years. Perthshire produced a number of different items including bowls, vases, glasses, plates and lamps. These were originally sold with Perthshire labels attached to the bottoms. None are known to contain a signature cane. Several pieces (number unknown) are marked with an impressed "P" on the base. One is shown below. Since labels can be removed or fall off, items from this line may appear unidentified, and in some cases, be misidentified as Monart, Vasart or Strathearn. A careful examination of the canes used in these designs should reveal the original maker.

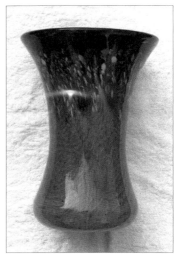

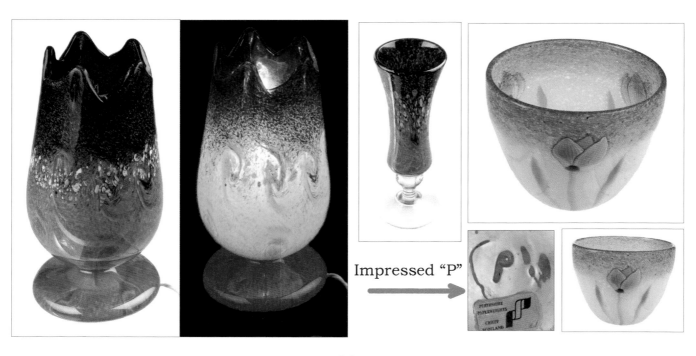

Impressed "P"

Perthshire Paperweights Collectors Club

In late 1997 Perthshire formed the Perthshire Paperweights Collectors Club. Neil Drysdale, Managing Director of Perthshire Paperweights Limited, became the Club Chairman. Upon joining, new members received an exclusive membership paperweight that had a "PPCC" center cane.

Benefits of membership included the introductory gift weight, an opportunity to buy Special Edition weights that were available only to members, advanced information on new Perthshire production designs, and a newsletter. The first Special Edition club weight was made in 1998, and new designs were made for 1999, 2000, and 2001. Members who renewed in 2000 received a special CD that included video clips of the Perthshire production process. A full multimedia CD was planned to be made and offered for general sale; however, it apparently was never produced.

Members who renewed or joined in 2001 received a Special Edition china mug with "Perthshire Paperweights" and the Perthshire Paperweights logo on one side and a picture of a Perthshire PP1 paperweight on the other.

In the fall of 2001, after Neil's untimely death, administration of the Club was transferred to Larry Selman of L.H. Selman Ltd. With the closing of Perthshire in January 2002 the club was also terminated.

INTRODUCTORY GIFT WEIGHT
Small weight with a large "PPCC" center cane surrounded by a ring of blue and white canes and eight pale green and orange radial twists separated by single pink and white daisy canes at the outer edge, all on an opaque teal ground. Each person who joined the Perthshire Paperweights Collectors Club received one of these weights as an introductory gift. Made 1998 through 2001.

FIRST ANNUAL COLLECTORS WEIGHT
A pink flower with green leaves surrounded by eight radial latticinio rods that separate eight three-flower nosegays and extend through an outer ring of canes, all on a black ground. Signed with the "PPCC" cane in the base and inscribed with the number of the weight. Made in 1998.

SECOND ANNUAL COLLECTORS WEIGHT
Two white flowers and an opening bud on a branch with dark green leaves on a translucent red ground. One top facet and five side facets. Signed with the "PPCC" cane in the base and inscribed with the number of the weight. Made in 1999.

THIRD ANNUAL COLLECTORS WEIGHT
A bouquet of pink and white flowers with green stems and leaves surrounded by a ring of canes on a translucent dark blue ground. One top facet and six side facets. Signed with the "PPCC" cane in the base and inscribed with the number of the weight. Made in 2000.

FOURTH ANNUAL COLLECTORS WEIGHT
A blue flower with buds on a long green stem with green leaves on a translucent dark amethyst ground. One top facet and six side facets. Signed with a "P" cane next to the stem and the "PPCC" cane in the base. Inscribed with the number of the weight. Made in 2001.

MUG
A large china mug with a picture of a PP1 paperweight on one side and a red and black "PP" logo and "Perthshire Paperweights" on the other side. The bottom of the mug bears the Highland China logo. The mug was given to collectors who joined or renewed their membership in 2001.

Picture Canes

New England Glass Company Running Rabbit

This section includes pictures of most (but probably not all) of the silhouette and colored picture canes that Perthshire produced over the years. As many different cane pictures as possible are shown, but not necessarily the variations found when similar or identical pictures were bundled with a different surround. In most cases the pictures show canes in weights; however, some pictures are from loose canes.

Silhouette and picture canes (also called figure canes) have long been considered as highly desirable extras in paperweights. From the early Venetian figures of Bigaglia to the Baccarat Gridels and the New England Glass Company "Running Rabbit," figure canes have had a prominent place in paperweight history.

There are two distinct—and quite separate—types of figure canes: the silhouette cane and the colored picture cane.

Silhouette canes are those that show an opaque (usually) single-color figure set against a contrasting surround. The Baccarat Gridels and the New England Running Rabbit are classic examples of silhouette canes. Although we typically visualize silhouettes as a dark or black image against a lighter or white background, these silhou-ettes do not have to be black on white. Any combination of a single-color figure set against a contrasting color qualifies. The Baccarat Red Devil

Baccarat Red Devil

is an example a silhouette cane that is not black and white. The New England Running Rabbit can be found as a black rabbit against a white surround or a white rabbit against black.

Colored picture canes can be much different than silhouette canes (or may be quite simi-lar, for example, the Perthshire black and white penguin colored picture cane). Typi-cally colored picture canes are much more complex and often

Perthshire penguin

include several colors. Examples of colored picture canes in an-tique paperweights include the flower canes found in some Baccarat weights, and the gondolas, human

Baccarat flower cane

faces and other pic-tures found in Bigaglia and some other Vene-tian weights.

Just as these two types of figure canes are quite different in appearance, the way

Venetian face

they are made can be quite different as well. Silhouette canes were typically made by pouring a single color glass into a figure-shaped mold, thereby casting the figure. This casting was then set into a second mold and the surround color was poured into the mold to form the com-pleted silhouette.

This method doesn't work with colored picture canes. Creating these highly complex and very colorful picture canes requires a completely different—and very time-consuming—process.

First, thin single-color rods, each about 1/2 to 1 millimeter in diameter, are pulled. These thin rods are then cut into long, but manageable lengths. The long rods are then scored and cut into 4-1/2 inch lengths. A wide variety of colors and shades must be made in order to reproduce the design accurately.

Pulling the fine rods

Cutting into long lengths

Scoring for length

Cut rods

Next, plasticine clay is applied to a steel plate and the surface is smoothed in preparation for applying a pattern. The pattern to be reproduced is selected and pressed onto the clay surface and then traced by hand. After the pattern is removed, the tracing indentations guide the insertion of the rods into the clay.

Smoothing the clay

The pattern to copy

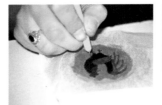

Tracing the pattern

Inserting rods

Inserting the thousands of rods individually takes a lot of time. The central design is completed first and then the surrounding color is applied. The surrounding color may use as many rods as the design itself. When all of the fine rods are in place, an outer ring of much thicker rods is applied.

Inserting rods into clay

Design taking shape

Nearly done

Inserting the outer ring

Before the picture cane can be heated for fusing, the clay must be cleaned off the end. The picture cane, wrapped with copper wire to hold it in place, is ready to be fused into one piece. The cane is placed in the oven and heated to 1004 degrees F. A pontil is then attached to the fused cane.

Cleaning off the clay

Ready to fuse

In the oven to fuse

Attached to a pontil

The copper wires are removed from around the cane. The heated cane is marvered to make it smooth and round. The end of the cane is trimmed off and the cane receives its final shaping.

Removing the wires

Marvering the cane

Trimming the end

Final shaping

After attaching a pontil to the trimmed end, the cane is pulled to the desired length. When pulling is finished, the cane is snapped to check the design inside. Lengths of the picture cane are then bundled with millefiori canes and prepared for fusing.

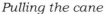
Pulling the cane

Finished pulling

The results

Bundling the cane

The final product is an accurate reproduction of the original pattern. In this example, the rooster picture cane is the center piece of the PP197 Limited Edition weight from 1998.

Final product

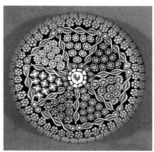
PP197 with rooster cane

Perthshire started experimenting with picture canes during their very first year in business. Several early examples are known; however, it wasn't until 1973 that picture canes were used as primary design elements in production weights. This resulted in a major increase in the number of designs created. Beginning with the 1973 designs and in the ensuing years, Perthshire created the largest variety of colored picture canes ever made by any one factory. In fact, it is quite probable that Perthshire made more different picture canes than all of the other paperweight factories combined, including those made for the antique weights by Baccarat, St. Louis, and others. Over 400 different picture canes are documented on pages 106 through 126. If the variations created by simply changing the surrounding ring of millefiori are added, the number goes well over 500!

In this section, as many of these different colored picture canes as possible are shown. There is no doubt that other examples exist that may or may not have been incorporated into weights, or were used only in samples or prototypes and never released to the public. This section shows variations of a common design in the picture itself; however, no attempt was made to show the variations created by simply changing the surrounding millefiori canes.

The pictures are grouped by category and then arranged alphabetically within that category. The major categories include:

Animals

Birds

Cartoon & Nursery Rhyme Characters

Christmas

Insects

Miscellaneous

People

Plants

Symbols

Transportation (Cars, Boats, Airplanes, Balloons, Train Engines, etc.)

Water Creatures (Fish, Frogs, etc.)

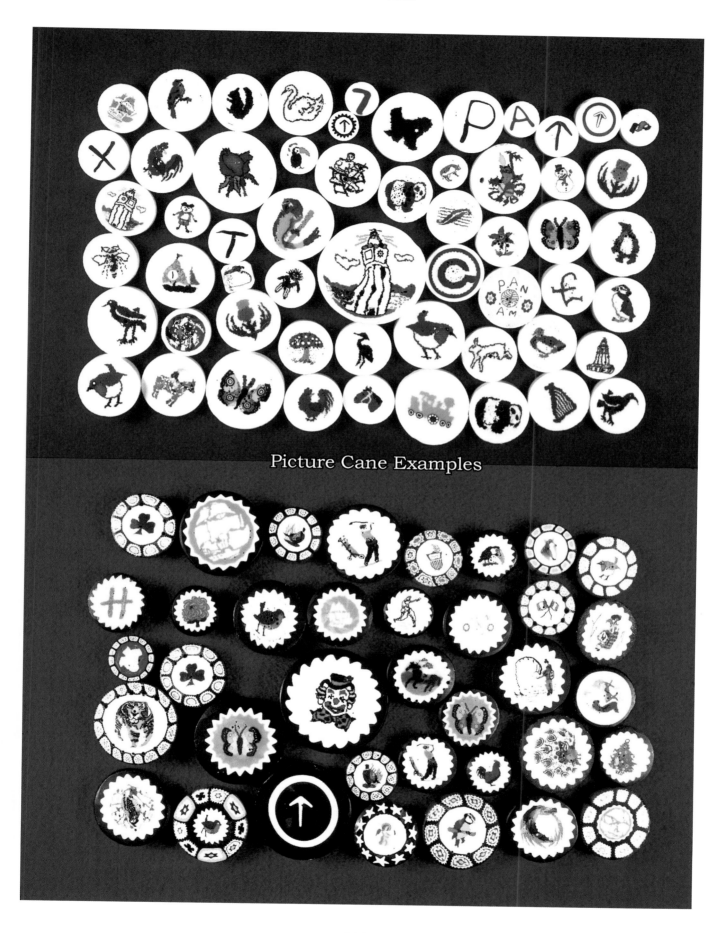

Picture Cane Examples

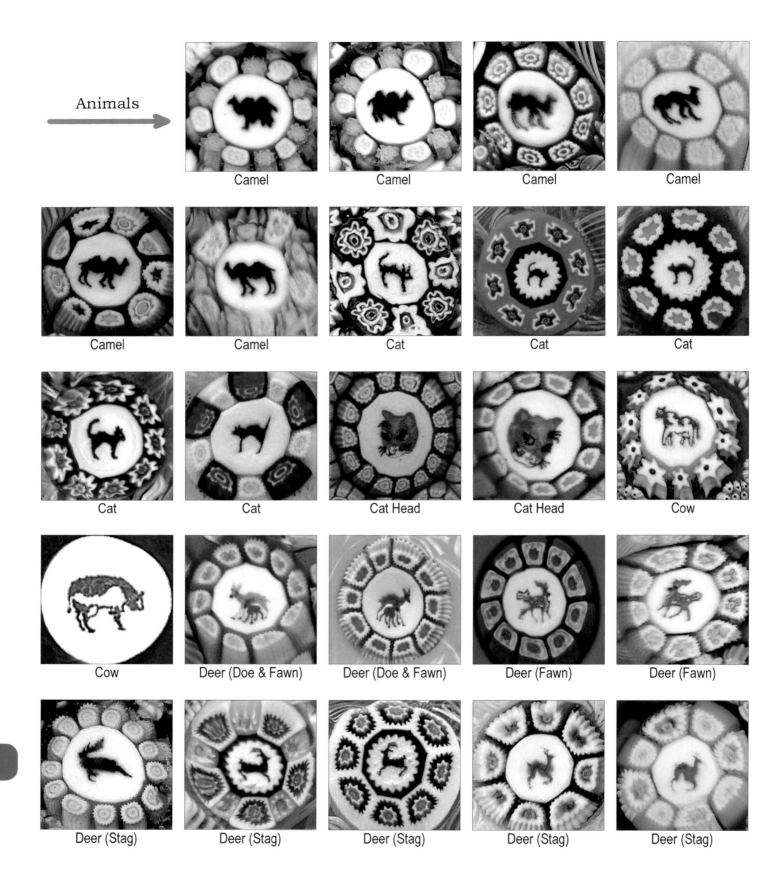

Animals →

Camel	Camel	Camel	Camel

Camel	Camel	Cat	Cat	Cat

Cat	Cat	Cat Head	Cat Head	Cow

Cow	Deer (Doe & Fawn)	Deer (Doe & Fawn)	Deer (Fawn)	Deer (Fawn)

Deer (Stag)	Deer (Stag)	Deer (Stag)	Deer (Stag)	Deer (Stag)

Dog (Collie)

Dog Head (Collie)

Dog (Dalmatian)

Dog (Dalmatian)

Dog (Dalmatian)

Dog (Dalmatian)

Dog (German Shepherd)

Dog (German Shepherd)

Dog (Scottie)

Dog (Scottie)

Dog

Dog

Dog (Terrier)

Dog (Terrier)

Elephant

Elephant

Elephant

Elephant

Elephant

Elephant

Elephant

Ermine

Ferret

Ferret

Gorilla

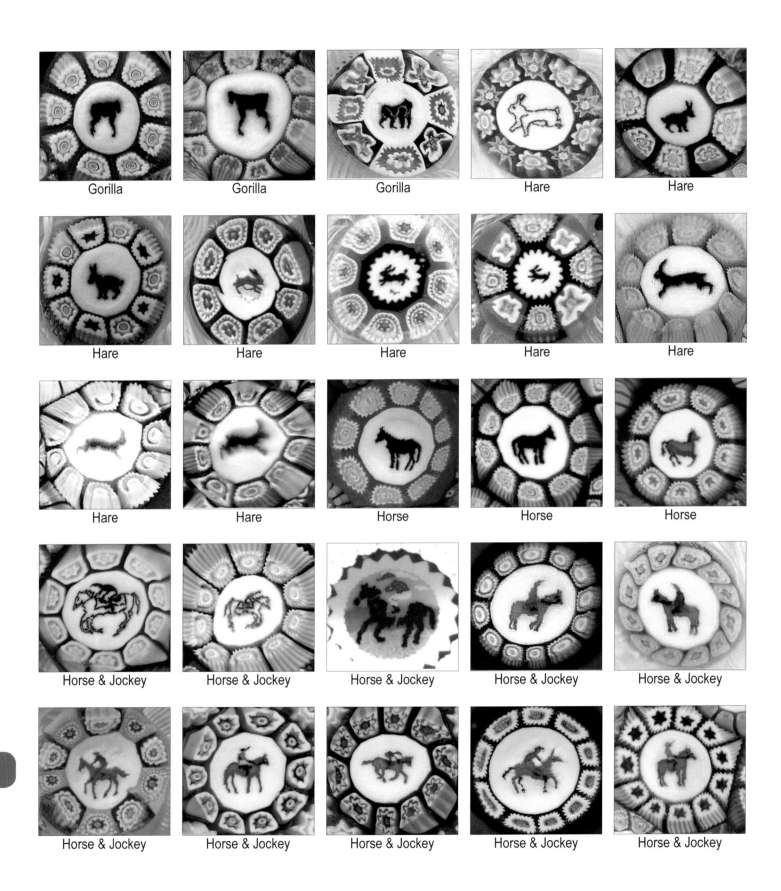

Gorilla	Gorilla	Gorilla	Hare	Hare
Hare	Hare	Hare	Hare	Hare
Hare	Hare	Horse	Horse	Horse
Horse & Jockey	Horse & Jockey	Horse & Jockey	Horse & Jockey	Horse & Jockey
Horse & Jockey	Horse & Jockey	Horse & Jockey	Horse & Jockey	Horse & Jockey

Horse & Rider   Horse & Rider   Horse & Rider   Pony Express   Horse Head

Horse Head   Horse Head   Horse Head   Kangaroo   Kangaroo

Kangaroo   Kangaroo   Kangaroo   Kangaroo   Lion

Lion   Mouse   Mouse   Mouse   Panda

Panda   Panda   Panda   Panda   Panda

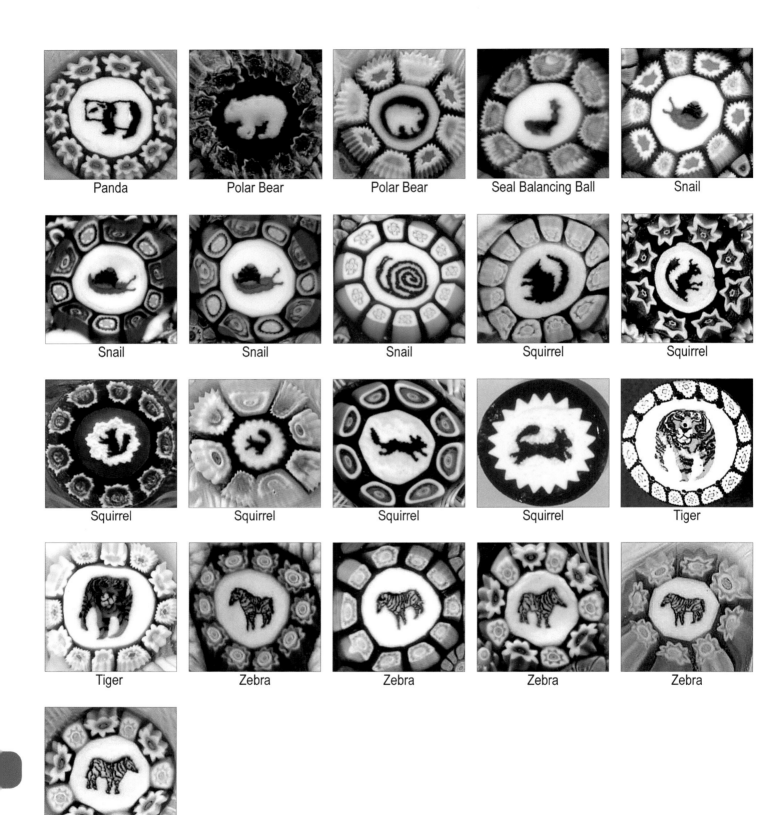

Panda

Polar Bear

Polar Bear

Seal Balancing Ball

Snail

Snail

Snail

Snail

Squirrel

Squirrel

Squirrel

Squirrel

Squirrel

Squirrel

Tiger

Tiger

Zebra

Zebra

Zebra

Zebra

Zebra

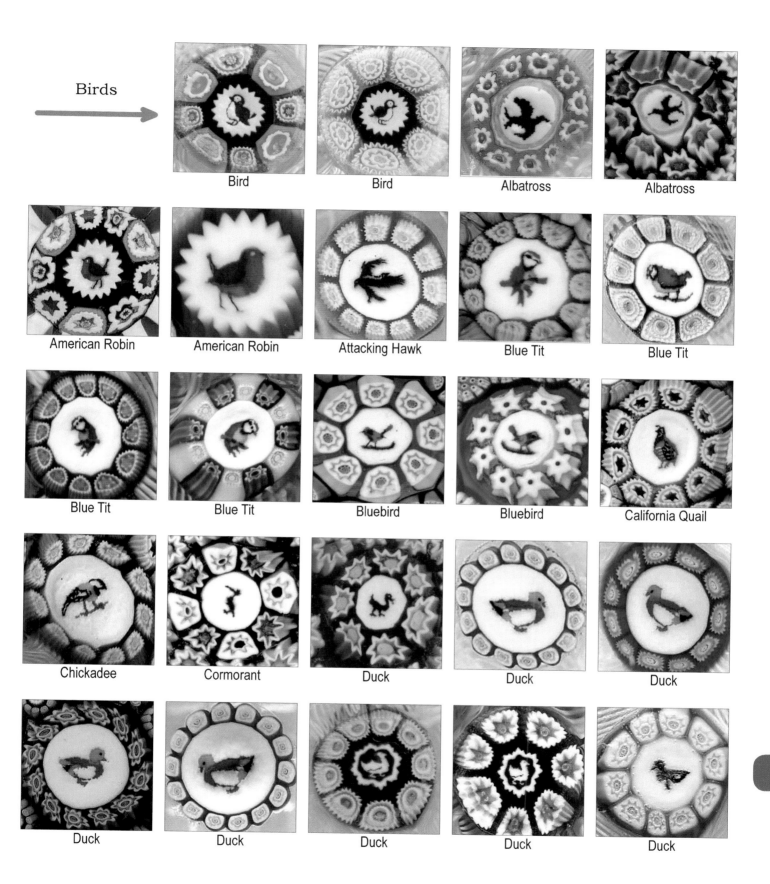

Birds →

Bird

Bird

Albatross

Albatross

American Robin

American Robin

Attacking Hawk

Blue Tit

Blue Tit

Blue Tit

Blue Tit

Bluebird

Bluebird

California Quail

Chickadee

Cormorant

Duck

Duck

Duck

Duck

Duck

Duck

Duck

Duck

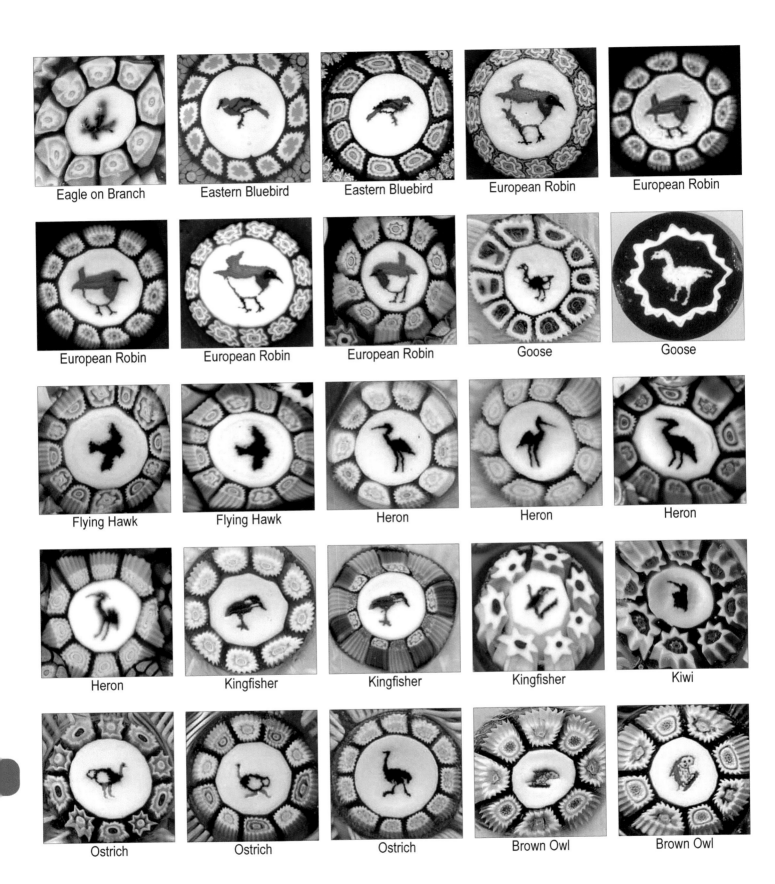

Eagle on Branch   Eastern Bluebird   Eastern Bluebird   European Robin   European Robin

European Robin   European Robin   European Robin   Goose   Goose

Flying Hawk   Flying Hawk   Heron   Heron   Heron

Heron   Kingfisher   Kingfisher   Kingfisher   Kiwi

Ostrich   Ostrich   Ostrich   Brown Owl   Brown Owl

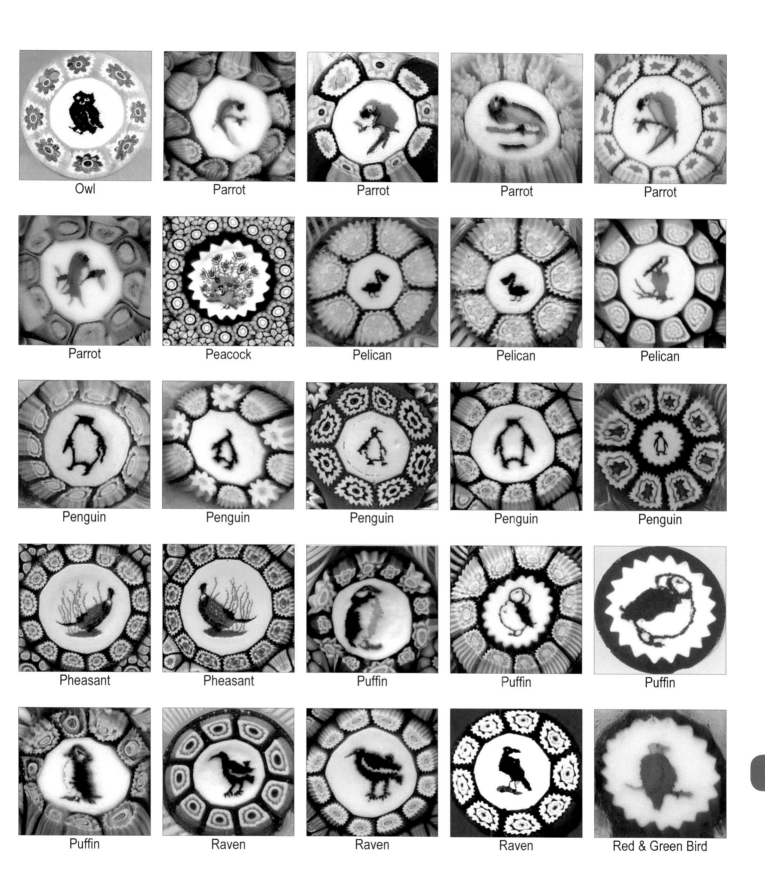

Owl	Parrot	Parrot	Parrot	Parrot
Parrot	Peacock	Pelican	Pelican	Pelican
Penguin	Penguin	Penguin	Penguin	Penguin
Pheasant	Pheasant	Puffin	Puffin	Puffin
Puffin	Raven	Raven	Raven	Red & Green Bird

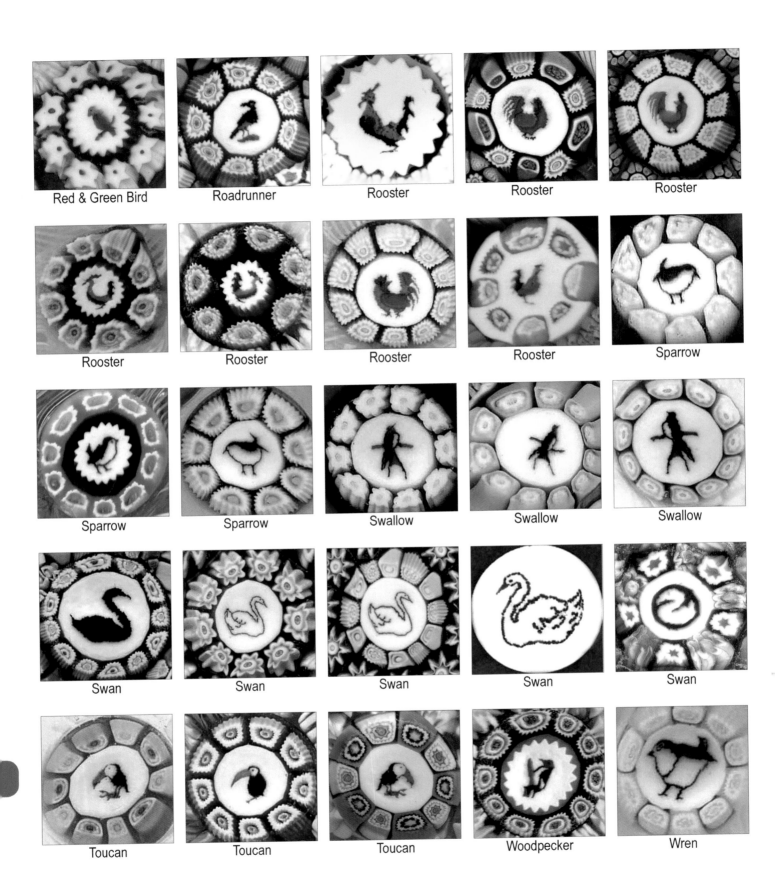

Red & Green Bird

Roadrunner

Rooster

Rooster

Rooster

Rooster

Rooster

Rooster

Rooster

Sparrow

Sparrow

Sparrow

Swallow

Swallow

Swallow

Swan

Swan

Swan

Swan

Swan

Toucan

Toucan

Toucan

Woodpecker

Wren

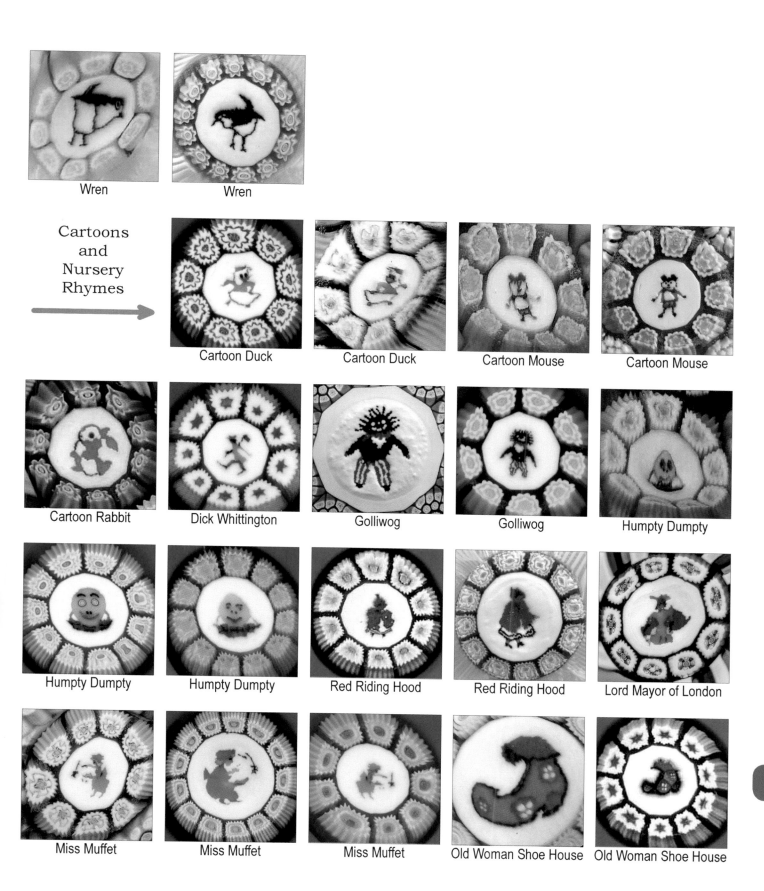

Wren

Wren

Cartoons and Nursery Rhymes →

Cartoon Duck

Cartoon Duck

Cartoon Mouse

Cartoon Mouse

Cartoon Rabbit

Dick Whittington

Golliwog

Golliwog

Humpty Dumpty

Humpty Dumpty

Humpty Dumpty

Red Riding Hood

Red Riding Hood

Lord Mayor of London

Miss Muffet

Miss Muffet

Miss Muffet

Old Woman Shoe House

Old Woman Shoe House

Old Woman Shoe House

Christmas

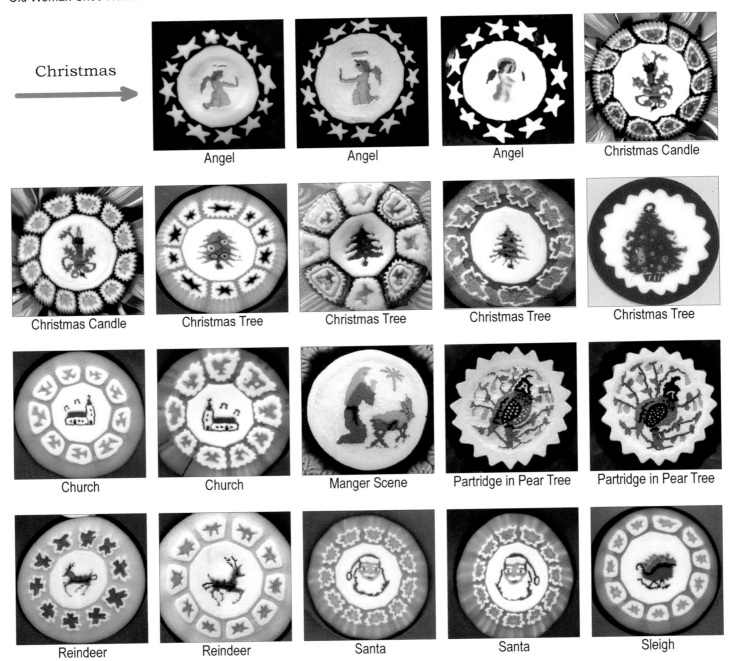

Angel	Angel	Angel	Christmas Candle
Christmas Candle	Christmas Tree	Christmas Tree	Christmas Tree	Christmas Tree
Church	Church	Manger Scene	Partridge in Pear Tree	Partridge in Pear Tree
Reindeer	Reindeer	Santa	Santa	Sleigh

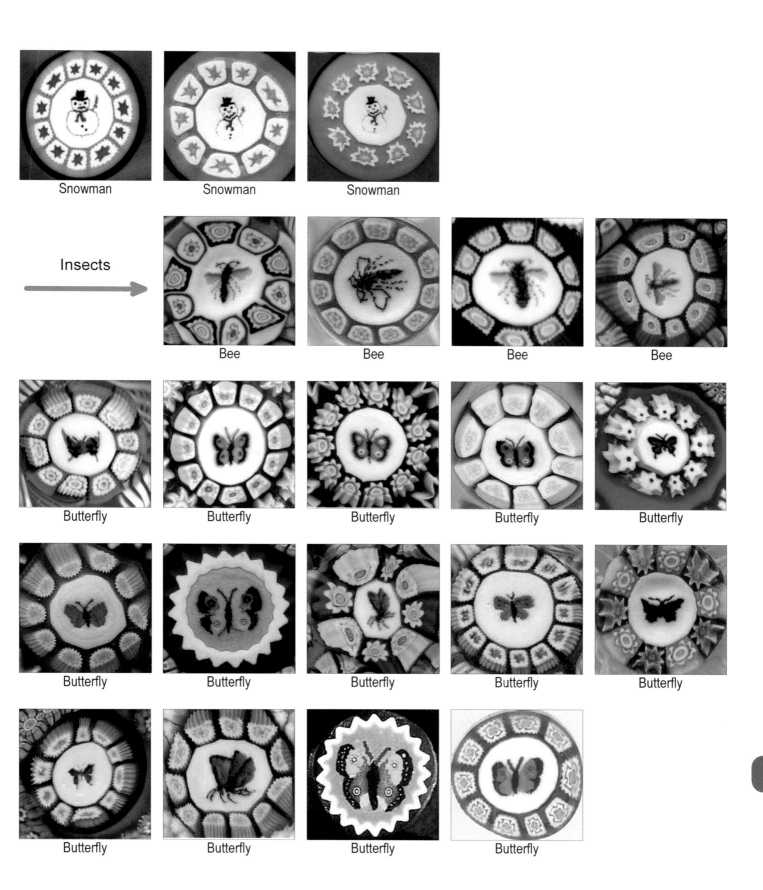

Snowman Snowman Snowman

Insects →

Bee Bee Bee Bee

Butterfly Butterfly Butterfly Butterfly Butterfly

Butterfly Butterfly Butterfly Butterfly Butterfly

Butterfly Butterfly Butterfly Butterfly

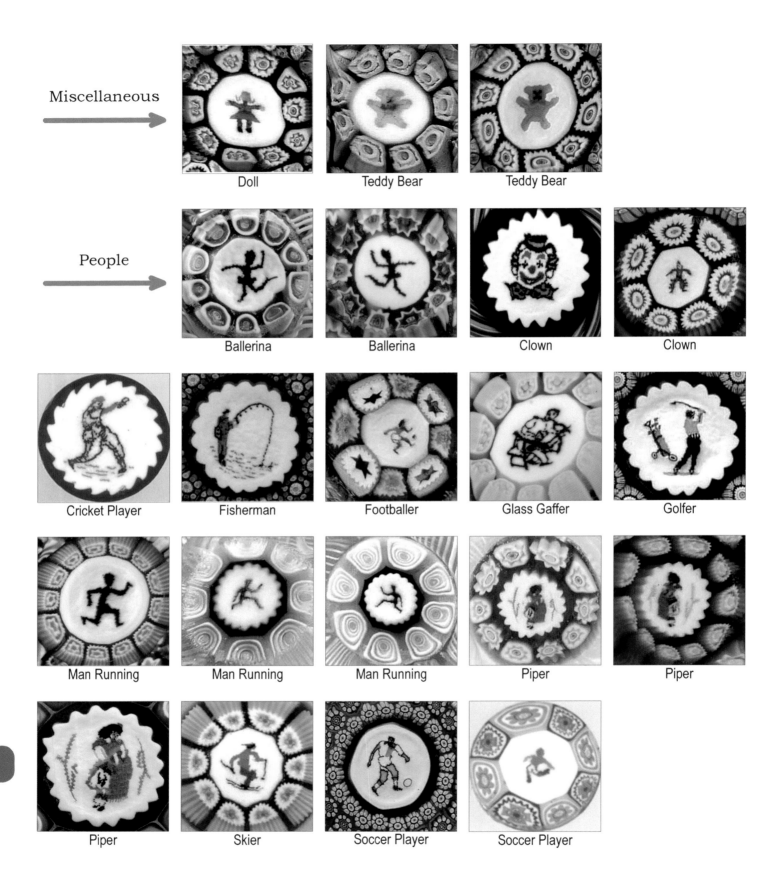

Miscellaneous →

People →

Doll

Teddy Bear

Teddy Bear

Ballerina

Ballerina

Clown

Clown

Cricket Player

Fisherman

Footballer

Glass Gaffer

Golfer

Man Running

Man Running

Man Running

Piper

Piper

Piper

Skier

Soccer Player

Soccer Player

Plants →

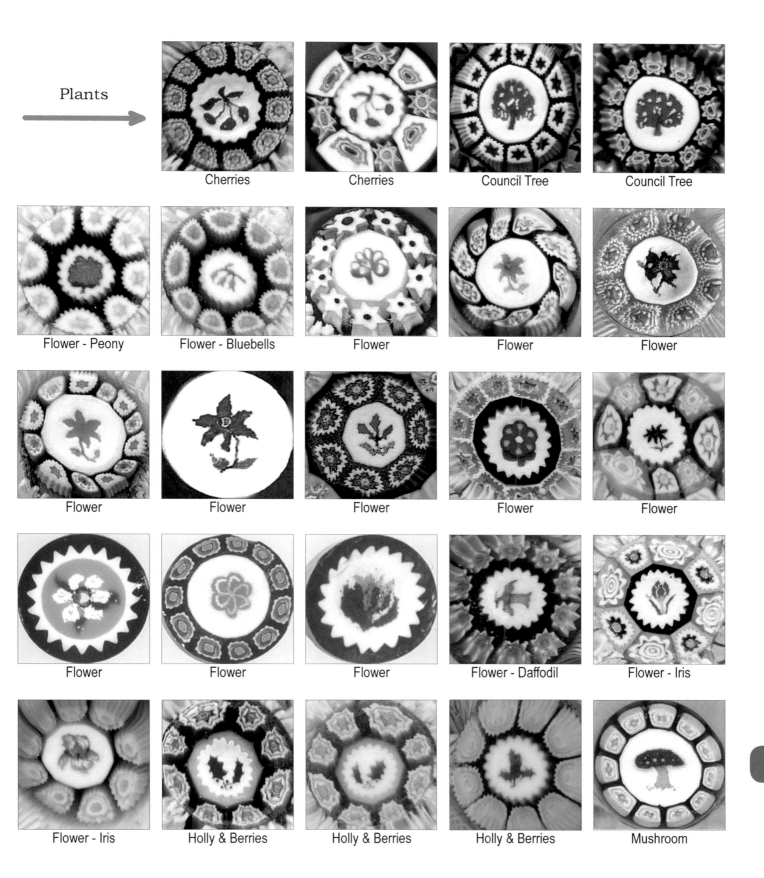

Cherries

Cherries

Council Tree

Council Tree

Flower - Peony

Flower - Bluebells

Flower

Flower

Flower

Flower

Flower

Flower

Flower

Flower

Flower

Flower

Flower

Flower - Daffodil

Flower - Iris

Flower - Iris

Holly & Berries

Holly & Berries

Holly & Berries

Mushroom

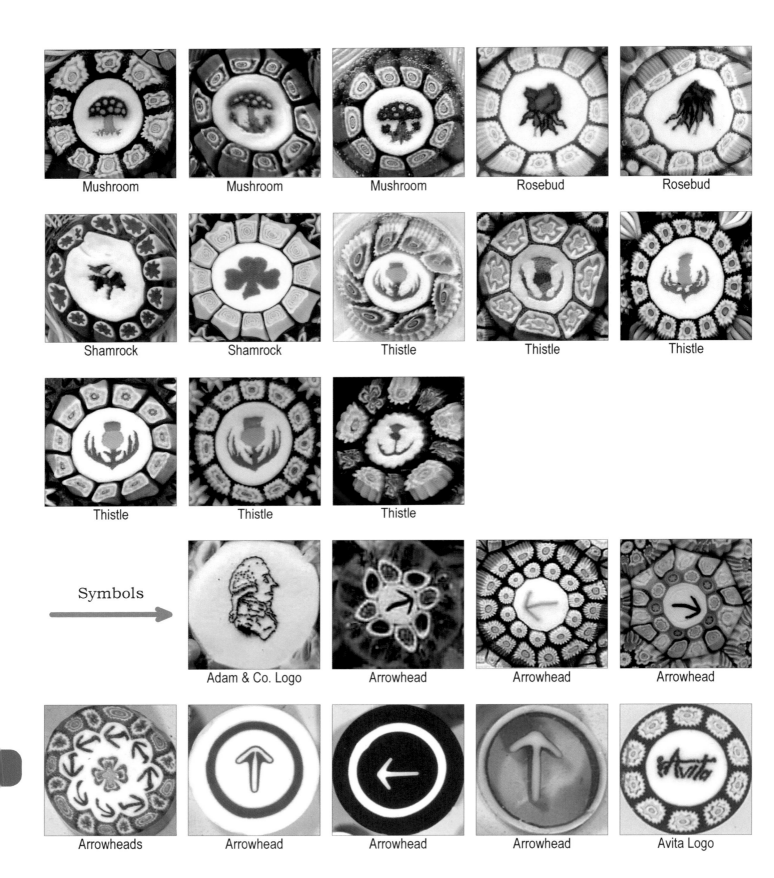

Mushroom	Mushroom	Mushroom	Rosebud	Rosebud
Shamrock	Shamrock	Thistle	Thistle	Thistle
Thistle	Thistle	Thistle		

Symbols →

Adam & Co. Logo	Arrowhead	Arrowhead	Arrowhead
Arrowheads	Arrowhead	Arrowhead	Arrowhead	Avita Logo

Club

Clydesdale Bank Logo

Crieff Gas Co. Logo

Royal Wedding Crown

Diamond

French Flags

Gavel

Glenside Organics Logo

Bell

Bell

Harp

Harp

Heart

Harrods of London Logo

Lighthouse

Lighthouse

Lighthouse

Moritex Corp. Logo

Music - Treble Clef

Musical Notes

Olympic Torch

Pan Am Logo

Paperweight Tour

Perthshire Logo

Pound Sign

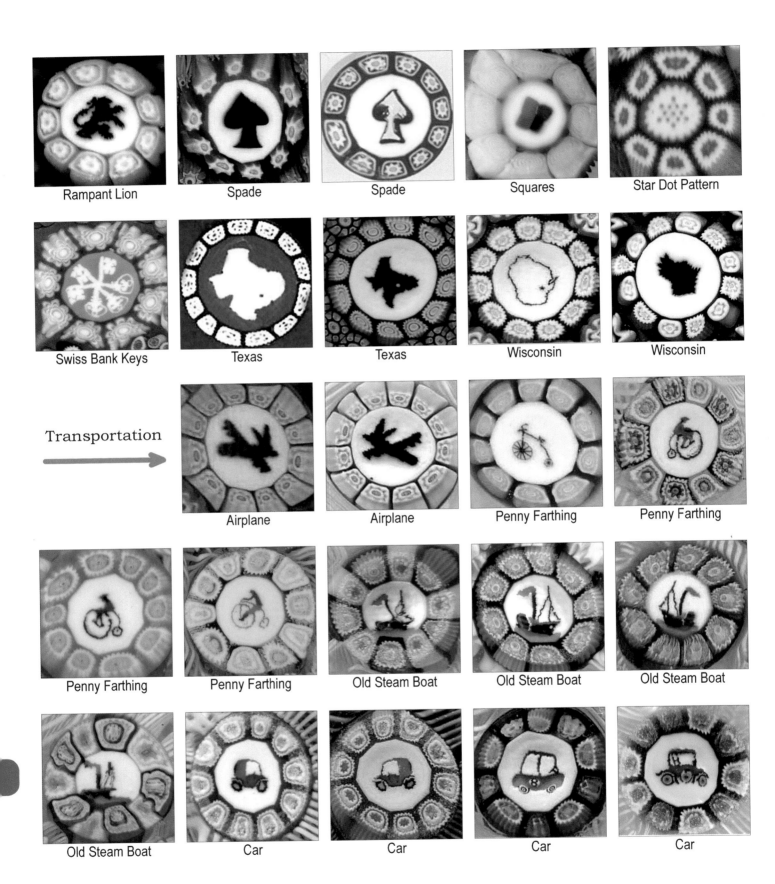

Rampant Lion   Spade   Spade   Squares   Star Dot Pattern

Swiss Bank Keys   Texas   Texas   Wisconsin   Wisconsin

Transportation   Airplane   Airplane   Penny Farthing   Penny Farthing

Penny Farthing   Penny Farthing   Old Steam Boat   Old Steam Boat   Old Steam Boat

Old Steam Boat   Car   Car   Car   Car

Dune Buggy   Dune Buggy   Dune Buggy   Old Car   Hot Air Balloon

Hot Air Balloon   Sail Boat   Sail Boat   Sail Boat   Sail Boat

Sail Boat   Sail Boat   Sail Boat   Sail Boat   Sail Boat

Sail Boat   Sail Boat   Spanish Armada Test   Spanish Armada   Spanish Armada

Old Steam Engine   Old Steam Engine   Train Engine   Train Engine   Train Engine

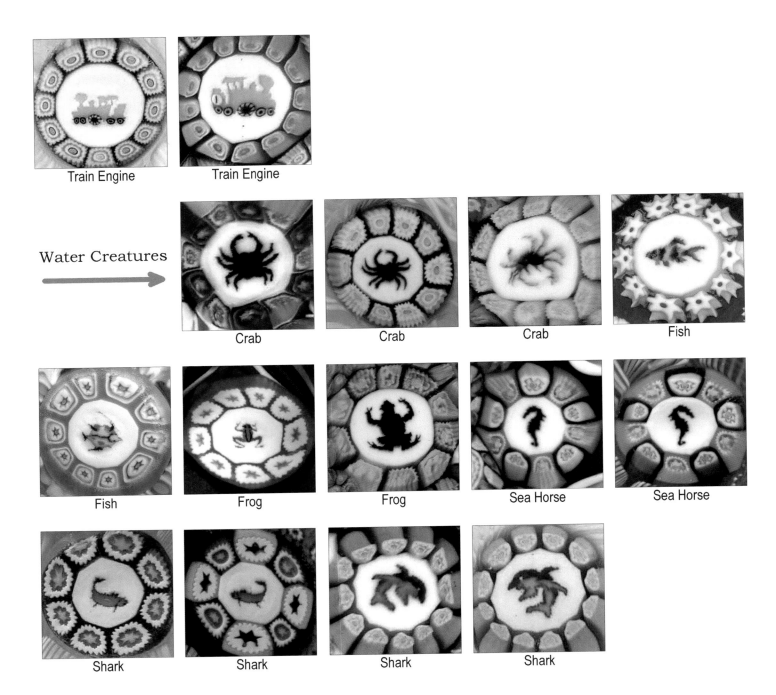

Train Engine Train Engine

Water Creatures

Crab Crab Crab Fish

Fish Frog Frog Sea Horse Sea Horse

Shark Shark Shark Shark

Scrapbook

This section is dedicated to the men and women of Perthshire Paperweights who worked every day to improve their capabilities and therefore the artistry of Perthshire Paperweights.

The Lochaline Sand Mine where Perthshire got its sand

The chemicals added to make the batch

Mixing the
chemicals to
make the batch

Shoveling the batch
into the furnace

Checking the quality of the glass

Placing canes in the
millefiori setups

A lampworker forming a flower

Completed picture cane before fusing

Removing the wires
from a fused picture
cane

Applying color
to the outside of
a gather of glass

The beginning of
a bottle

Shaping a bottle

133

Turning the crank on a machine to make latticinio rods

Polishing the bottom of a weight

Johne Parsley instructing Perthshire employees

Quality
Control

The rejects

All that work........   (Sigh)

Characteristics Important for Identification

Type
Millefiori
Lampwork
Millefiori/Lampwork Combined

Size (diameter at the widest point)
Sizes are approximate
Miniature: less than 2 inches
Small: 2 inches
Medium: 2-1/2 inches
Large: 3 inches
Magnum: over 3-1/2 inches

Shape
Domed or Faceted
Pressed: fluted or lobed
Upright, Pedestal (Piedouche), Footed
Other: knobs, bottles, dishes, etc.

Bases   (see previous book)
Flat and Polished
Fire-polished
Hollow-ground
Cutting (if any)

Special Designs
Christmas
Commemorative
Souvenir

Design Features
Hollow
Ground Type: lace, latticinio, clear, translucent color, opaque color
Overlay: flash (translucent) or opaque (single, double, or triple)

Pattern or Design of the Setup
Number and Arrangement of Flowers, Canes, etc.
Special Canes
Crown

Color
Setup
Ground
Base
Overlay

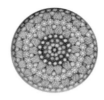

*Millefiori
(PP193)*   *Lampwork
(1999F)*   *Combination
(1998E)*

*Domed
(PP232)*   *Faceted
(2001H)*   *Fluted
(PP171)*

*Upright
(PP239)*   *Pedestal
(2001G)*   *Footed
(1999G)*

Identification

The process of identification provides answers to the following two questions:

Was the weight made by Perthshire?

If it was, which weight is it?

Some of the steps used to answer the first question are the same as those used to answer the second. The simple, four-step process below, when used with the information in the remainder of this section, should lead to the answer to both questions.

1. Look for a date or signature.

2. Note all of the physical characteristics.

3. Carefully analyze the design and cane group patterns.

4. Look through the appropriate sections of the book to find a pattern/design match.

Using this process should result in positive identification of more than 95 percent of all Perthshire weights, even the one-of-a-kind pieces.

Signatures and Dates

Was it made by Perthshire? Perhaps the easiest way to answer this question is to look for a signature or signature/date cane. If you don't find one, other characteristics of the weight must be examined closely.

Nearly all Perthshire paperweights contain either a cane with the letter "P" in it, or, alternatively, a cane with a "P" that includes a date. In a few cases, Perthshire used a "PP" with the date. The numbers making up the date are in individual canes in some early weights.

The signature cane is often found in the center of the design or on the underside of the weight. However, it may be incorporated into the design, perhaps in the outer ring of canes or even hidden somewhere in the setup, such as in the middle of a flower. This is especially true when the ground is clear. Occasionally the signature is not a cane, but just the letter "P" inscribed on the bottom surface or on the side near the bottom of the weight.

Scratch-signed "P"

Examples of "P" canes with dates

Examples of "P" canes

CAUTION: The "P" signature has been used by other paperweight makers. Pairpoint and Johne Parsley are but two of the possible signatures that may be confused with the Perthshire "P."

On rare occasions, Perthshire weights bear not only the factory signature, but also that of the artist. As an example, several magnum millefiori weights, including the 2001 Millefiori Ball, contain "PMcD" signature canes (for Peter Mc-Dougall) in the design.

Perthshire sometimes inscribed the edition number on the base of the weight in addition to dating it. A few weights have a certificate number and no other identification.

At the end of this section, there is a multi-page chart showing the production years for Limited Edition and General Range weights and the years in which design changes occurred. This chart can be used to limit the range of possibilities if you have a dated weight.

Characteristics and Style

If the weight has no signature or date, the next step is to determine if it looks like a Perthshire. With the millefiori weights, this is not as difficult as it sounds. As you page through this book or the earlier Perthshire book, you will see the style and "feel" of the Perthshire canes and layouts.

Canes and Twists. Unlike the canes in antique weights, specific cane characteristics such as the number of cogs are not specific to the factory. However, Perthshire canes have several characteristics that contribute to the Perthshire style.

Perthshire is known for its complex canes made by bundling many simple canes together. Whether simple or complex, Perthshire canes are typically very well formed. Even the most complex canes are extremely precise. Most weights also include twist canes or strips of latticinio. These often extend from the center to the outer edge, *i.e.*, radially, and divide groups of canes into segments with a specific pattern. Many weight designs use simple eight-pointed star canes to outline or fill in pattern areas.

Simple canes (PP243)

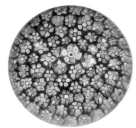

Complex canes (PP220)

While most of the simple canes exhibit common characteristics, the complex canes are of almost limitless patterns.

Beginning collectors sometimes find Murano or Chinese millefiori weights and assume that, because they are millefiori,

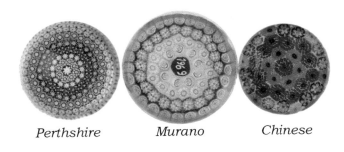

Perthshire　　　*Murano*　　　*Chinese*

they might be Perthshire. However, once a comparison is made between the types of canes, the collector is quick to recognize that there is really no comparison as far as the quality, detail, size, and color of the canes.

Perthshire incorporated picture canes, both silhouette and colored, into many of its designs. Silhouettes are shapes filled in with a single color (either molded or made by stacking rods), while picture canes are made by stacking many rods of various colors to make a full-color or black and white picture. When examined with a magnifying glass, the edge irregularities from the glass rods are visible. You can quickly learn to recognize many of these canes as being uniquely Perthshire. These specialty canes offer an opportunity to develop an interesting subcollection.

Grounds. Quite often the canes and twists are placed on a color ground, either opaque or translucent. With very few exceptions, Limited Edition weights have a ground of lace or translucent color. General Range weights often have an opaque ground.

Bases. After approximately 1974, most Perthshire weights were made with a hollow-ground base. Pictures of the various bases and cuttings are shown in *The Complete Guide to Perthshire Paperweights.*

The Perthshire Style. The best way to get a sense of the Perthshire style is to look at a large number of Perthshire weights, or the pictures in this book or *The Complete Guide to Perthshire Paperweights* until the commonality forms an image in your memory. This will also help you to recognize the picture and silhouette canes that Perthshire has used.

Lampwork weights and weights with a combination of lampwork and millefiori do not exhibit this "feel" as much, but, fortunately, almost all Perthshire lampwork or combination millefiori/lampwork weights are signed.

Which Perthshire Weight Is It?

One approach would be to page through this book or the earlier book until you find a match, but remember that colors vary in many Perthshire Limited Edition and General Range weights , even though the design remains the same. Some combinations of colors, particularly in millefiori designs, can make the appearance so different that misidentification, or even no identification, occurs. There is a better way.

Weights with Signatures and Dates. The task is greatly simplified if you find a signature with a date. You can then proceed to the various categories of the Catalogue and find the range of weights made in that year. In the case of Limited Edition and General Range weights, the easiest way to identify the possible PP numbers is to use the chart at the end of this section, which shows production years for all designs with PP numbers.

Next, look at the characteristics of the weight. It will have a combination of physical characteristics that will quickly identify it. Important characteristics are listed on the chart at the beginning of this section.

Signed Weights with No Date. If you find a signature, but no date, especially in a millefiori weight, you probably have a "PP Something" weight. Use the physical characteristics listed on the chart at the beginning of the section to determine what type of weight you have. *Size is very important.* Next, study the design. What is unique about it?

Look carefully at the layout. Are there twist canes that separate the millefiori canes into pie-shaped segments? Do the twists, if any, only radiate out from the center, or are they laid out in a pattern or a ring around the center?

Next look closely at the pattern of the millefiori cane groups. Counting out from the center, decide what specific pattern you see. Are the canes between the radials in a 1-1-2-3, a 1-2-3-3, or some other pattern? See the example shown on page 40 in the Catalogue for help in describing patterns.

Now, armed with the specifics of the weight, go through this book and the previous book until you find a specific match. Remember that colors vary and can be deceiving. Colors are not specific to a given design unless they are stated in the description.

Cautions and Caveats

Differences in colors and faceting, while sometimes helpful, can be misleading.

Colors, both of the ground and of the millefiori or lampwork, are often not specific as to design. A pattern may stand out much more in some combinations of colors than it does in other color combinations.

Faceting can alter the appearance of a

PP169 weights in different color combinations

weight dramatically. Some weights were issued in both faceted and domed versions. For example, the PP237 is domed and the PP237A is the identical pattern,

PP237, domed   *PP237A, faceted*

but faceted. When color and faceting variations are combined, a dramatic difference in appearance can result. It is therefore necessary to look closely to identify patterns.

A strange or unidentifiable pattern, while possibly an indication of a somewhat unique weight, may be just a variation of a regular pattern. The factory setup teams occasionally added an extra twist or a few extra canes to a design. These minor variations within a design concept are usually called design variations and have no affect as to either the collectibility or value of the piece. Only the Limited Edition weights and the Annual Collection weights are absolutely (almost) true to the design. General Range weights do, although not often, vary slightly from the standard designs.

In summary

1. Look for a date or signature.

2. Note size and all of the other physical characteristics.

3. Carefully analyze the design and cane group patterns.

4. Look through the appropriate categories of the Catalogue to find a pattern/design match.

Steps 1 to 3 will let you quickly eliminate

all of the weights which do not fit as to size, date, significant features or canes, etc., and will lead you to the proper parts of the Catalogue to facilitate quick identification.

Weight Identification Examples

Example 1: You have a large (3-inch diameter) weight with a translucent green color ground, a center rooster picture cane surrounded by a ring of canes, seven radial twists (radiating from the center) that separate cane groups of 1-2-3-4, then a ring of twist segments separated by pairs of canes and two outer ring of canes, and a "P1998" cane in the base (underside).

By going to the chart of production years

Example 3: You have a large weight with a bouquet of three small red flowers, several radiating leaves and stems with buds. The weight has a top facet and two rows of five side facets each, a star-cut base, and a scratch-signed "P" on the base.

for Limited Edition and General Range weights and finding the range of PP numbers for weights made in 1998, you find that the description of the PP197 design fits exactly.

Example 2: You have a medium-sized (2-1/2 inch diameter) weight with a black ground, fourteen twists radiating from three rings of canes around a center cane and separating single canes at the outer end of the twist, then a ring of canes. It is signed with a "P" cane in the center. By looking through the book you can easily determine that you have a PP62.

Looking in the Annual Collection category (since this is a lampwork weight), it is necessary to browse through the pictures since the weight is undated. Observation shows a similarity to the picture of the 2001F weight pictured.

Limited Edition and General Range Production Years

	1969	1970	1971	1972	1973	1974	1975	1976	1977	1978	1979	1980	1981	1982	1983	1984	1985	1986	1987	1988	1989	1990	1991	1992	1993	1994	1995	1996	1997	1998	1999	2000	2001	2002
PP1	x	x	x	x	x	x	x	x	x	c	x	x	x	c	x	x	x	x	x	x	x	x	x	x	x	x	x	x	x	x	x	x	x	x
PP2	x	x	x	x	x	x	x	x	x	c	x	x	x	x	x	x	x	x	x	x	x	x	x	x	x	x	x	x	x	x	x	x	x	x
PP2A																																		x
PP3	x	x	x	x	x	x	x	x	x	x	x	x	x	x	x	c	x	x	x	x	x	x	x	x	x	x	x	x	x	x				
PP4	x	x	x	c	x	x	x	x	x	x	x	x	x	x	x	c	x	x	x	x	x	x	x	c	x	x	c	c	x	c	c	c	x	x
PP5	x	x	x	c	x	x	x	x	x	x																								
PP6	x	x	x	c	x	x	x																										x	x
PP7	x	x	x																															
PP8	x	x	x																															
PP9	x	x	x																															
PP10	x	x	x	x	x	x	x	x	x	x	x	x	x	x	c	x	x	x	x	x	x	x	c	c	x	x								
PP11	x	x	x	c	x	x	x	c														x	c	c										
PP12	x	x	x	x	x	x	x	c	x	x	x																							
PP13	x	x	x	x	x	x	x	x	x	x	x	x	x	x	x	x	x	x	x	x	x	x	x	x	x	x								
PP14	x	x	x	x	x	x	x	x	x	x		x	x	x	x	x	x	x	x	x	x	x	x	x	x	x	x	x	x	x	x	x	x	x
PP15	x	x	x	x	x	x	x	x	x	x																								
PP16	x	x	x	x	x	x	x																											
PP17	x	x	x	x	x	x	x	x	x	x	x	x	x	x	x	x	x	x	x	x	x	x	x	c	x	x	x	x	x	x	x	x	x	x
PP18	x	x	x	x	x																						x	x	x	x	c	c	x	x
PP18A																											x	x	x	x	x	x	x	x
PP18B																											x	x	x	x	x	x	x	x
PP18C																											x	x	x	x	x	x	x	x
PP19	x	x	x	x	x	x	x	x	x	x	x	x	x	c	x	x	x	x	x	x	x	x	x	c	x	x	x	x	x	x	x	x	x	x
PP19A																																		
PP20		x	x	x	x	x	x	x	x	x	x	x	x	x	c	x	x	x	x	x	x	x	x	x	x	x	x	x						
PP21		x							x	x	x	x	x	x	x	x	x	x	x	x	x	x	x	x	x	x								
PP22					x	x	x																											
PP23					x	x	x																											
PP24				x		x	x																											
PP25						x	x																											
PP26						x																												
PP27							x	x	x	c																								
PP28							x	x	x	x	x	x	x	x																				
PP29							x	x																										
PP30								x	x	x	x																							
PP31								x	x	x	c	c	c	c	c	c	c	c	x	x														
PP32										x	x	c	c	c	c	c																		
PP33										x	x	x																						
PP34										x	x	x																						
PP35											x	x																						
PP36											x																							
PP37												x																						
PP38												x																						
PP39												x																						
PP40												x	x																					
PP41																x	x	x	x	x	x	c	x	c	x	x								
PP42																			c	x	x	x	x	x	x	x	x	x	c	x	x			
PP43													x	x	x	x	x	x	x	x														
PP44													x																					
PP45													x	x	x	x	x	c	x	x	x	x	x	c	x	x	x	c	c	x	x	c	c	c
PP46													x	x	x	x	x	x	x	x	x	c	c	x	c	c	c	c	c	c	c	c	c	
PP47													x	x		x	x	x	x	x	x	x	x	x	x	x								
PP48																																		
PP49													x	x																					
PP50														x																				
PP51	not issued												x	x	x	x	x	x	x	x	x	x	x	x	x	x	x							
PP52													x	x	x	x	x	x	x	x	x	x	x	x	x	x								
PP53														x	x																			
PP54															x												x							
PP55	not issued															x	x	x	x	x	x	x	x	c	x	x								
PP56																x	x	x	x	x	x	x	x	x	x	x	x	x	c	x	x	x	x	x
PP57																x	x	x	x	x	x	x	x	x	x	x	x	x	x	x	x	x	x	x
PP58																x	x	x	x	x	x	x	x	x	x	x	x	x	x	x	x	c	x	x
PP59																x	x	x	x	x	x	x	x	x	x	x	x							
PP60																x	x	x	x	x	x	x	x	x	x	x	x	x	x			x	x	x
PP61																	x	c	x	x	x	x	c	c	c	c	x	x	x			x		
PP62																c	c	c	c	c	c	c	c	c	c	c	c	c						
PP63															x	c																			
PP64															x																				
PP65														x																				
PP66																																		

Note: **x** indicates weight made that year; **c** indicates a design change that year

Limited Edition and General Range Production Years

	1969	1970	1971	1972	1973	1974	1975	1976	1977	1978	1979	1980	1981	1982	1983	1984	1985	1986	1987	1988	1989	1990	1991	1992	1993	1994	1995	1996	1997	1998	1999	2000	2001	2002
PP67															x	x																		
PP68															x	x																		
PP69															x	x																		
PP70															x	x	x																	
PP71																x																		
PP72																x																		
PP73																x																		
PP74																	x	x	x	x	x	x	x	x	x	x	x	x	x	x	x	x	x	x
PP75																x	x	x	x	x														
PP76																	x	x	x	x	x	x	x	x	x	x	x	x	x	x	x	x	x	x
PP77																	x	x	x	x	x	x	x	x	x	x	x	x	x	x	x	x	x	x
PP78																	x	x																
PP79																		x																
PP80																	x																	
PP81																	x	x	x	x	x	x	x	c	x	c	c	c	c					
PP82																	x	x	x	x	x	x	x	x	c	c								
PP83																	x	x	x	x	x	x	x	x	c	x								
PP84																	x	x	x	x	x	x	x	x	x	x	x	x						
PP85																	x	x	x															
PP86																		x	x															
PP87																		x	x	x	x						c	c						
PP88																		x	x	x	x						c	x						
PP89																			x	x	x						c	x						
PP90																			x	x	x	x												
PP91																			x	x	x	x	x	x	x	x	x	x	x	x	x	c		
PP92																			x	x	x	x	x	x	x									
PP93																			x	x	x	x	x	x	c	x	x	x	x	x	x			
PP94																			x	x	x	x	x	x	x	x	x	x	x	x	x			
PP95																			x	x	x	x	x	x	c	x	x	x	x	x	x	c		
PP96																			x	x	x													
PP97																			x															
PP98																			x	x														
PP99																				x														
PP100																				x														
PP101																				x														
PP102																				x														
PP103																				x														
PP104																				x														
PP105																				x														
PP106																				x														
PP107																					x													
PP108																					x	x	x	x	x	x	x	x	x					
PP109																					x	x	x	x	x	x	x	x	x	x				
PP110																					x	x	x	x	x	x	x	x	x	x				
PP111																				x	x		x											
PP112																					x													
PP113																					x													
PP114																					x													
PP115																					x													
PP116																					x													
PP117																						x												
PP118																						x												
PP119																						x	c	x	x	x	x	x	x	x	x			
PP120																						x	x	x	x	x	x	x	x	x	x			
PP121																						x												
PP122																							x	x	x	x	x	x	x	x	x			
PP123																							x	x	x	x	x	x	x	x	x		x	x
PP124																							x	x	x	x	x	x	x	x	c		x	x
PP125																							x	x	x	x	x	c	c	x	x			
PP126																							x												
PP127																							x												
PP128																							x												
PP129																							x												
PP130																							x												
PP131																							x												
PP132																							x												
PP133																							x	x	x	x								
PP133A																							x	x	x	x								
PP134																										x	x							
PP135																							x	x										
PP136																							x	x										

Note: **x** indicates weight made that year; **c** indicates a design change that year

Limited Edition and General Range Production Years

	1969	1970	1971	1972	1973	1974	1975	1976	1977	1978	1979	1980	1981	1982	1983	1984	1985	1986	1987	1988	1989	1990	1991	1992	1993	1994	1995	1996	1997	1998	1999	2000	2001	2002
PP137																																		
PP138																							X											
PP139																							X											
PP140																							X											
PP141																								X										
PP142																								X										
PP143																								X										
PP144																								X										
PP145																								X										
PP146																								X										
PP147																								X										
PP148																									X									
PP149																									X									
PP150																									X									
PP151																									X									
PP152																									X									
PP153																									X									
PP154																									X									
PP155																										X		X	X					
PP156																												X						
PP156A																												X	c	X				
PP157																										X								
PP158																										X								
PP159																										X	X							
PP160																										X	X							
PP161																										X	X							
PP162																										X	X	X	X	X	X	X	X	X
PP163																											X							
PP164																											X							
PP165																																		
PP166																											X							
PP167																																		
PP168																											X							
PP169																											X	X	X	X	X	X	X	X
PP170																												X	X	c	X	X	X	X
PP171																																		
PP172																												X	X					
PP173																												X	X					
PP174																												X	X					
PP175																												X	X					
PP176																												X	X					
PP177																														X	X	X	X	X	X
PP178																														X	X	X	X	X	X
PP178A																														X					
PP179																														X					
PP180																														X					
PP181																														X					
PP182																														X					
PP183																														X					
PP184																														X					
PP185																															X				
PP186																															X	X	X	X	X
PP187																															X	X	X	X	X
PP187A																															X	c			
PP188	not issued																																	
PP189	not issued																																	
PP190	not issued																																	
PP191																														X				
PP192																														X				
PP192A																														X				
PP193																														X				
PP194																														X				
PP194A																														X				
PP195																														X				
PP195A																														X				
PP196																														X				
PP197																														X				
PP197A																														X				
PP198																															X			
PP199																															X			
PP200																																		

Note: **x** indicates weight made that year; **c** indicates a design change that year

Limited Edition and General Range Production Years

	1969	1970	1971	1972	1973	1974	1975	1976	1977	1978	1979	1980	1981	1982	1983	1984	1985	1986	1987	1988	1989	1990	1991	1992	1993	1994	1995	1996	1997	1998	1999	2000	2001	2002
PP200A																																		
PP201																																		
PP202																															X			
PP202A																															X			
PP203																															X			
PP203A																															X			
PP204																															X			
PP204A																															X			
PP205																															X			
PP206																															X			
PP206A																															X			
PP207																															X			
PP208																															X			
PP209																															X			
PP210																															X			
PP210A																															X			
PP211																															X			
PP212																															X			
PP213																																X		
PP213A																																X		
PP214																																X		
PP215																																X		
PP216																																X		
PP216A																																X		
PP217																																X		
PP218																																X		
PP219																																X		
PP220																																X		
PP221																																X		
PP222																																X		
PP223																																X		
PP224																																X		
PP225																																X		
PP226																																X		
PP227																																	X	
PP228																																	X	
PP228A																																	X	
PP229																																	X	
PP230																																	X	
PP231																																	X	
PP231A																																	X	
PP232																																	X	
PP233																																	X	
PP234																																	X	
PP235																																	X	
PP236																																	X	
PP237																																	X	
PP237A																																	X	
PP238																																	X	
PP239																																	X	
PP240																																	X	
PP241																																	X	
PP242																																	X	
PP243																																		X
PP243A																																		X
PP244																																		X
PP244A																																		X
PP245																																		X
PP246																																		X
PP247																																		X
PP248																																		X
PP249																																		X

Note: **x** indicates weight made that year; **c** indicates a design change that year

Glossary

Many of the glossary terms have examples cited. For weights not shown in this book, a reference is given to the previous book, *The Complete Guide to Perthshire Paperweights*.

ANNEAL. To lower the temperature of a newly formed weight by placing it in an oven which is cooled slowly over many hours. (At Perthshire this was about 24 hours.) This reduces the internal stress in the glass which could cause the weight to crack at some later time.

ANNEALING OVEN. See ANNEAL. The oven into which hot weights are placed to allow them to cool slowly.

ANNUAL COLLECTION WEIGHTS. Specially designed weights that were made in limited quantities for a specific year. Example: 1998A.

BARBER POLE. A weight in which the individual canes are separated by lengths of white latticinio rods containing one or more colored threads. See also CHECKER. Example: 1993C (in previous book).

BASAL RIM (BASE RIM). The outer ring of the bottom of a weight with a concave base. The BASAL RIM contacts the surface on which the weight rests.

BASE. The underside or bottom of a weight.

BASKET. A cup or bowl shape made of staves, stretched millefiori canes or latticinio strips, above or into which the primary design element is placed. Example: 2000A.

BATCH. The term used to describe the mixture of sand and other ingredients to be melted to make glass.

BEEHIVE FACETING. See HONEY-COMB FACETING.

BOUQUET. A group of flowers placed together to form the setup. It may be flat or three-dimensional. Examples: flat – 1998B; three-dimensional – 1999F.

CANE. A single rod of glass containing a pattern that is visible from the side (TWIST CANE) or in cross-section (MILLEFIORI CANE). **Also:** A short slice or piece from either a millefiori cane or a twist cane used as one of the elements in a millefiori design. As used in the Catalogue section of this book, the word CANE refers to a slice of millefiori cane used as an element in the SETUP or design. The term TWIST is used to refer to twist canes.

CANE CLUSTER. A small group of millefiori canes, typically used as part of a design. Example: PP195.

CARPET GROUND. A ground formed of many identical millefiori canes set close together. Example: PP195.

CHECKER (CHEQUER). A pattern where the individual millefiori canes are separated by strips of colored glass (rods) or latticinio canes. Example: 1991C (in previous book).

CHESSBOARD. A pattern of adjacent squares. Example: PP35 (in previous book).

CLEAR GROUND. A gather of clear glass used as a ground. When viewed, the setup appears to be floating in the clear glass. Example: 2001A.

CLOSE CONCENTRIC. A pattern of concentric rings of canes, each ring touching or nearly touching the adjacent rings. See also CONCENTRIC and OPEN CONCENTRIC. Example: PP156A.

CLOSE MILLEFIORI. Millefiori canes placed very close together so as to touch or nearly touch. The term can apply to an area of a weight or to a ring of canes. See also CLOSEPACK. Example: 2000B.

CLOSEPACK. Many millefiori canes placed so as to touch or nearly touch, completely covering a part of or the entire design area of the weight. See also CLOSE MILLEFIORI.

CLUSTER. See CANE CLUSTER.

COG CANE. A cane with "teeth" or ridges around the perimeter.

COLORED PICTURE CANE. See PICTURE CANE.

COLOR GROUND. A layer of colored glass used to form the ground. May be OPAQUE, TRANSLUCENT or TRANSPARENT. Sometimes has a mottled appearance if colored chips are fused together.

COMPLEX MILLEFIORI CANE. A cane made by combining several simple canes or groups of canes and then fusing them together to form a complex pattern within a single cane. Example: PP220.

CONCENTRIC. A pattern made from rings of canes, one within the next, all having a common center point. Example: PP3.

CRIMP. A tool made from metal and shaped to form a rose or other design form within a weight when pressed into the hot glass.

CRIMP WEIGHT. A weight containing a design made using a CRIMP. Example: PP133A (in previous book).

CROWN WEIGHT (CROWN). A weight with ribbons, latticinio twists, or rods, or any combination thereof, running from the top center outward and down the sides to the bottom. Example: PP232.

CUSHION. A ground on which the setup is placed. It is usually somewhat dome-shaped (convex) and can be made of latticinio or colored glass. Example: 1999G.

CUTTING. The finishing of the outside of a weight by grinding facets or decorative designs into the surface. A star-cut pattern on the bottom of a weight is one type of cutting. Example: 1998B.

DATE CANE. A cane with a date in it referring to the year of production or the date of an event being commemorated. It can be a single cane, or individual canes for each numeral fused together. See page 139.

DESIGN. The overall layout or pattern of the weight, including the interior elements and the surface cutting. See also MAIN DESIGN ELEMENT.

DIAMETER. The widest measurement across the horizontal direction of the weight. This is the most common measurement used to determine the size of a weight.

DIAMOND CUT. Two sets of parallel cuts on the base of the weight that cross at a angle of other than 90 degrees to form many small diamond shapes. See also GRID CUT, FEATHER CUT, and STRAWBERRY CUT.

DOME. Convex surface of the upper part of the weight. The curvature of the DOME magnifies the setup.

DOMED WEIGHT. A weight with an upper surface that is smoothly curved and not faceted. Example: PP21.

DOUBLE (OR TRIPLE) OVERLAY. See OVERLAY.

ENCASE. To surround the setup with molten glass.

ENCASED OVERLAY. A weight with a layer of clear glass completely surrounding a smaller overlaid weight within. The inner weight and the outer layer of clear glass are usually cut with fancy patterns. Example: 1998 Special Limited Edition.

END-OF-DAY WEIGHT. So named from the practice of taking whatever canes and pieces that were left over at the end of the day and combining them all into a randomly patterned weight. See also: SCRAMBLED WEIGHT. Example: PP19.

FACET. A flat or concave window cut into the surface of the weight, thereby changing the magnification of the setup when viewed through the faceted area. Sometimes also called a PRINTY.

FEATHER CUT. A combination of a GRID or DIAMOND cut and a STAR CUT. This results in a bottom design where the raised areas between the rays of the star have a GRID or DIAMOND pattern, giving the appearance of a feather.

FINGER CUT (FINGER FACETS). See FLUTE.

FIRE POLISH. To use a torch or flame to melt a glass surface thereby smooth-

ing it. Fire polishing is often used to smooth the sharp edges of the PONTIL MARK after the weight is broken off the PONTIL ROD.

FLASH. A layer of TRANSPARENT or TRANSLUCENT colored glass placed on the surface or base of a weight. It is often used as an overlay and then partly cut away by faceting. Example: 1998G.

FLAT BOUQUET. Two or more two-dimensional flowers placed together to form the main design element. See also NOSEGAY and THREE-DIMENSIONAL BOUQUET. Example: 1998B.

FLOATING DESIGN. A design placed well above the ground or basket. Example: 1998C.

FLOWER WEIGHT. A weight which has a single large flower as the main design feature. Example: 2000C.

FLUTE. An elongated cut placed vertically on the side of a weight. See also FINGER CUT. Example: PP171.

FOOT. A wide flat piece attached to and extending out from the base of a weight or a pedestal. Example: 1999G.

FURNACE. A gas or electric heating unit containing the POT where the BATCH is melted to make glass.

GARLAND. A ring of canes or small lampwork pieces that surrounds and accents the MAIN DESIGN ELEMENT. The ring can also be shaped to form lobes or loops. The garland itself can be the MAIN DESIGN ELEMENT. Two or more lobed (looped) garlands can be intertwined to form a complex garland. Example: 1998D.

151

GATHER. A quantity of molten glass obtained by dipping the PONTIL ROD into the POT containing the glass. The GATHER is used to pick up or encase the setup, to fill MOLDS to make millefiori CANES, or for a variety of other uses.

GENERAL RANGE WEIGHTS. Weights which were issued in unlimited quantities, usually over several years. Examples: PP1, PP2, PP3.

GRID CUT. Two sets of many parallel cuts set at 90 degree angles to make small squares. See also DIAMOND CUT, FEATHER CUT, and STRAWBERRY CUT.

GROUND. The layer of glass below the main design. Some types of grounds are MOSS, CARPET, LACE, LATTICINIO, COLOR, and CLEAR.

HOLLOW-GROUND BASE. The bottom of a weight where the PONTIL MARK has been ground away leaving a concave bottom with a BASAL RIM around the perimeter.

HOLLOW WEIGHT. A weight which has a hollow interior within which the main design element (usually a three-dimensional element) is placed. Example: 1998G.

HONEYCOMB CANE. A cane that has a honeycomb appearance. Example: 1988B (in previous book).

HONEYCOMB FACETING. All-over small facets that cause the internal design to appear many times at the surface of the weight. Also called BEEHIVE FACETING. See also GEOMETRIC FACETING. Example: 1989F (in previous book).

INK BOTTLE. A bottle containing a millefiori or lampwork design in the bottom and in the stopper. Perthshire stopped making bottles after 1997. Example: PP83 (in previous book).

INK WELL. See INK BOTTLE.

INTERTWINED (INTERLACED) GARLANDS. Two or more GARLANDS interlaced to form a complex pattern. An INTERTWINED trefoil GARLAND results in a pattern with six lobes – three from each trefoil. Each GARLAND is continuous and usually of a single type of cane. Sometimes called Entwined Garland. See also LOOPED GARLAND. Example: 1978E (in previous book).

LACE GROUND. A ground made of jumbled latticinio pieces to give an appearance of lace. Also known as "Upset Muslin." Example: 1998E.

LAMP. A burner or torch that uses gas and oxygen. Lampworkers use this burner to melt or soften small pieces of glass so that they can be hand-formed into flowers, animals, etc.

LAMPWORK. A design element made by forming individual parts over a LAMP and then joining them together to form the finished motif.

LARGE WEIGHT. A weight with a diameter of about 3 inches. See also MAGNUM.

LATTICINIO. Clear glass rods containing white or other solid colored glass threads which have been twisted (usually) during the PULL.

LATTICINIO GROUND. Pieces of latticinio laid out either patterned or jumbled to form a ground. See LACE GROUND and SPIRAL LATTICINIO.

LIMITED EDITION WEIGHTS. Weights made in a quantity of not more than a preset limit during one or more years. See ANNUAL COLLECTION WEIGHTS. Example: PP192.

LOOPED (LOOP) GARLAND. One or more garlands which are shaped to form loops or lobes. Example: 1980G (in previous book).

MAGNUM. A weight with a diameter of more than 3-1/2 inches. Perthshire literature refers to some weights smaller than 3-1/2 inches in diameter as "magnum." Classic antique weights larger than 3-1/4 inches in diameter are called magnum.

MAIN DESIGN ELEMENT. The lampwork motif or millefiori design that is the primary design of the paperweight.

MARVER. A smooth flat steel plate which is used to shape a gather of molten glass. By rolling the gather back and forth (marvering), the glass is formed into a smooth cylinder. The gather may also be rolled in colored glass powder to add color to the cylinder.

MEDIUM WEIGHT. A weight approximately 2-1/2 inches in diameter.

MILLEFIORI. From the Italian words for "Thousand Flowers." A cane formed from various colors of glass, such that its cross-section resembles a flower.

MILLEFIORI CANE. See CANE.

MINIATURE WEIGHT. Weight with a diameter of less than 2 inches. Note that with regard to the ANNUAL COLLECTION WEIGHTS, Perthshire used the term "miniature weight" to indicate that they were of a small size compared to full-sized weights. ANNUAL COLLECTION WEIGHTS called "miniature" can be over 2 inches in diameter.

MOLD. A metal shape into which molten glass is pressed.

MOSS GROUND. A ground of green canes with many individual rods within each cane to give a moss-like appearance. Example: 1976E (in previous book).

MOTIF. The main design of a weight.

MUSHROOM. An encased group of millefiori canes, usually of closepack or concentric pattern, which has long canes at the perimeter. These long canes are pulled down and to the center to form a stem. When viewed from the side, the design has a mushroom shape. Example: 2000F.

MUSLIN GROUND. See LACE GROUND.

NEWEL POST FINIAL. Large weight mounted on a metal (usually) base intended to be attached to a post at the end of a staircase.

NOSEGAY. A FLAT BOUQUET in which millefiori canes are used as flowers set on leaves. Example: 1977A (in previous book).

ONE-OF-A-KIND. A weight that is unique as to design, cutting, and/or color. See PROTOTYPE.

ONE-OFF. A term sometimes used to refer to a ONE-OF-A-KIND weight.

OPAQUE. Not allowing light to pass through. It is not possible to see through OPAQUE glass. See also TRANSLUCENT and TRANSPARENT. Example: 1999A.

OPEN CONCENTRIC. A concentric pattern where the adjacent concentric rings are spaced apart from each other. Canes within each ring may be close or spaced. See CONCENTRIC and CLOSE CONCENTRIC. Example: PP32L (in previous book).

OVERLAY WEIGHT. A weight with one or more layers of colored glass applied to the surface, then partially removed by cutting and faceting. A SINGLE OVERLAY has one layer of colored glass applied to the surface. In this book SINGLE OVERLAY refers to an OPAQUE layer. A FLASH overlay has a single layer of TRANSLUCENT or TRANSPARENT colored glass applied. A DOUBLE OVERLAY typically has a layer of white glass with a layer of some other color over it. When cut, both the colored and white layers are exposed. A TRIPLE OVERLAY (by far the least common) has a colored layer applied, then a white (usually) layer, and finally another colored layer. When cut, all three layers become visible. See also ENCASED OVERLAY. Examples: Flash Overlay – 1998G; Single Overlay – 1993F (in previous book); Double Overlay – 1998B; Triple Overlay – 1977C (in previous book).

PAPER KNIFE. Letter opener.

PATTERNED MILLEFIORI WEIGHT. A weight in which millefiori canes, and often twists, are used to create a geometric internal design.

PEDESTAL WEIGHT. Also called a PIEDOUCHE. A weight placed on top of a column or stem of glass. This stem can be thick or thin, and is often decorated with latticinio strips, a pattern formed into the glass stem, torsades, etc. The pedestal may have a foot. Example: 2001G.

PICTURE CANE. A cane where the cross-section reveals an image of a picture or silhouette. See SILHOUETTE CANE.

PIEDOUCHE. French term for PEDESTAL. See PEDESTAL WEIGHT.

POMPON CANE. A complex millefiori cane made from many curved segments that give an appearance of a many-petaled flower. Similar to, but more complex than a Clichy-type rose. Example: 1982G (in previous book).

PONTIL. See PONTIL ROD.

PONTIL MARK. A mark on the bottom of a weight where it was attached to a metal rod (PONTIL ROD) while it was being formed.

PONTIL ROD. A hollow metal rod used to gather molten glass from the POT and also to hold an object while it is being formed. Sometimes referred to as a PUNTY.

POT. A ceramic container inside of the furnace into which the BATCH is placed to be melted into glass. After melting, the pot holds the molten glass in the furnace.

PP. Designation for the GENERAL RANGE and LIMITED EDITION weights made by **P**erthshire **P**aperweights Limited.

PRESSED WEIGHT. A weight which has been pushed into a shaped MOLD while the glass is still soft, resulting in a cog-like or scalloped perimeter. Examples: PP163, PP170, PP171.

PRINTY. See FACET.

PROTOTYPE. A weight produced as a step in creating a design which would become a production weight. PROTO-TYPES, while probably ONE-OF-A-KIND weights, were not created with the intent of making only one weight of that design, but rather as a step leading up to a final, fully developed design for factory production.

PULL. A single length of millefiori cane made by stretching a thick, short rod while it is hot. This pull or cane is then cut into short lengths to be used in making complex canes or is sliced for use in making millefiori designs.

PUNTY. See PONTIL ROD.

RADIAL TWIST. A length of twist cane laid out like a spoke in a wheel. Example: PP108.

RIBBON. A flattened glass rod that usually has a different color on each side with white in between. When twisted, it is often used as an element of a CROWN WEIGHT. Example: PP232.

ROD. A piece of round, single-colored glass which can be used to form STAVES or to make part of a design. Example: PP230.

SCATTERED MILLEFIORI. A weight with individual millefiori canes randomly spaced in the weight. Example: PP13 (1975) (in previous book).

SCRAMBLED WEIGHT. A weight made using whole and broken millefiori canes and/or twists in no set pattern. See END-OF-DAY WEIGHT. Example: PP19.

SCRATCH SIGNED. A signature scratched onto the surface of the weight with a diamond pen, usually on or near the bottom. See page 139.

SETUP. The millefiori design made up of individual canes before they are encased in a weight. **Also:** The LAMPWORK parts after they are assembled and before they are encased.

SIGNATURE CANE. A CANE containing the initials of the factory (usually "P" or rarely "PP" for Perthshire) or the individual artist who made the weight. Perthshire signature canes come in several forms, both with and without dates incorporated in them. See page 139.

SILHOUETTE CANE. A CANE containing the filled-in outline of an object or animal, in a single color that contrasts with the surrounding area of the cane. See PICTURE CANE.

SIMPLE MILLEFIORI CANE. A MILLEFIORI CANE where all elements have a common center. See COMPLEX MILLEFIORI CANE. Example: PP243.

SINGLE OVERLAY. See OVERLAY WEIGHT.

SMALL WEIGHT. A weight approximately 2 inches in diameter. See also MINIATURE WEIGHT.

SPACED MILLEFIORI. A weight where the individual millefiori canes are separated by some distance. Example: PP47 (in previous book).

SPECIAL EDITIONS. Weights made to commemorate some special event such as the French Revolution, or at the request of a customer such as the Bergstrom-Mahler Museum of Glass. **Also:** A very limited series of weights made using very complex and difficult techniques such as DOUBLE OVERLAY ENCASED DOUBLE OVERLAY weights. **Note:** SPECIAL EDITION weights did not appear in the annual catalogues published by Perthshire. The Catalogue section contains a category on Special Edition weights.

SPIRAL LATTICINIO. Colored threads wrapped around a flattened core to form a cushion. See LATTICINIO and page 8.

SPOKE. A length of twist or latticinio laid out like a spoke in a wheel. See: RADIAL TWIST. Example: PP94.

STAR CUT. A pattern cut into the bottom of a weight to resemble a many-pointed star. The cuts may be of different lengths or different sizes and shapes.

STARDUST CANE. A cane made from many small, identical, star-shaped CANES. It is usually white, but can be any other single color.

STAVE. A LATTICINIO or colored glass ROD or CANE placed around the outside of a design and pulled down to form a BASKET.

STAVE BASKET. A basket shape made of RODS or CANES into or above which the SETUP is placed. See BASKET. Example: 2000A.

STRAWBERRY CUT. A fancy cutting on the bottom of a weight. Three sets of parallel cuts, placed at 120 degree angles, are made to form many small triangles and hexagons.

SUPER-MAGNUM. A weight with a diameter greater than 4 inches.

SWIRL CUT. Deep grooves that are cut into the surface of a weight and swirl from the bottom to the top of the weight. May be a clear or an overlaid weight. Example: 1987B (in previous book).

SWIRL WEIGHT. A weight with flattened rods placed close together, then twisted to form a pinwheel effect. May be used as the main design or as a ground. Example: 1998F.

THREE-DIMENSIONAL BOUQUET. A flower bouquet where each flower is formed in three dimensions. See also FLAT BOUQUET. Example: 1999F.

TORSADE. A ring made from a single TWIST joined at the ends to form a continuous piece. It encircles the design and may be placed inside or outside of a weight Example: 2000 Special Limited Edition.

TRANSLUCENT. Allowing light to pass. Fine detail cannot be distinguished when viewed through a TRANSLUCENT layer. If detail can be observed through a colored layer, it is often called TRANSPARENT. See also OPAQUE. Example: PP46 Heart.

TRANSPARENT. Clear (colorless) or with color that allows fine detail to be distinguished when viewed through it. See TRANSLUCENT and OPAQUE. Example: 1980B.

TWIST (TWIST CANE). A cane made by encasing colored glass rods within clear glass, then twisting the cane during the pulling or stretching process. See RIBBON.

UPRIGHT BOUQUET. A bouquet of three-dimensional flowers or fruits set in a vertical layout.

WHIMSY. A fanciful device, object, or creation especially in writing or art. Anything playful or fanciful, as an artistic creation. An artistic rendering of a practical item.

Notes

Notes

Notes

About the Authors

After the Perthshire factory closed in 2002, the authors began working on their second Perthshire book to document the weights made during the period from the end of the first book, *The Complete Guide to Perthshire Paperweights*, (1997) to the end of the factory production in January 2002. The book was outlined, most of the photos were taken and much of the text was written. Then personal issues interrupted the progress. Marge and Gary McClanahan, who had been paperweight dealers when the first book was written, found their business had become even more active due to online sales. Debby and Colin Mahoney both became managers at their business location. Their increased workloads greatly reduced their free time until their retirements in 2011. So the book lay dormant. In 2014 the authors decided it was time to complete the book. After months of writing and re-writing text, and photographing and re-photographing items, the long-awaited sequel is done – and the authors are still friends.

We know this publication describing Perthshire's work from mid-1997 until the factory closed has been long anticipated. We hope it was worth the wait!